Starting Science ... Again?

Starting Science ... again?

Making Progress in Science Learning

Martin Braund

Los Angeles • London • New Delhi • Singapore • Washington DC

SAGE Publications Ltd
1 Oliver's Yard
55 City Road
London EC1Y 1SP

SAGE Publications Inc.
2455 Teller Road
Thousand Oaks, California 91320

SAGE Publications India Pvt Ltd
B 1/I 1 Mohan Cooperative Industrial Area
Mathura Road
New Delhi 110 044

SAGE Publications Asia-Pacific Pte Ltd
33 Pekin Street #02-01
Far East Square
Singapore 048763

Library of Congress Control Number: 2008933209

British Library Cataloguing in Publication Data

A catalogue record for this book is available from the British Library

ISBN 978-1-84787-008-7
ISBN 978-1-84787-009-4 (pbk)

Typeset by C&M Digitals (P) Ltd., Chennai, India
Printed in Great Britain by the Cromwell Press, Trowbridge, Wiltshire
Printed on paper from sustainable resources

To Stephen and Hannah.
May the transitions in your lives be smooth and trouble free.

Contents

Preface: A Tale of Two Entrants

Amin and Lisa went to different primary schools but in September they both went up to the same high school, Woodtown Comprehensive. Amin's primary school was in a small village. There were only 30 children in the school so his Year 6 (Y6) classmates (aged 10 or 11) were mixed with children from two other year groups; Year 4 (Y4 aged 8 or 9) and Year 5 (Y5 aged 9 or 10). Lisa's primary school was much larger having 350 children and was located in a housing estate on the edge of a large town. In Lisa's school, there were two classes containing just Y6 children.

Like most children of their age, Amin and Lisa were looking forward to the move to secondary school. It was not that they did not like their primary schools or their teachers there; it was more a sense of growing up – a sort of graduation point, if you like. Of course, they had worries and fears too. Both Amin and Lisa were worried about being lost in such a big place and they thought they might get picked on or bullied by older children. Some children in their schools had older brothers and sisters at Woodtown and they told them horror stories about how strict the teachers were and how if you did not do your homework all sorts of horrible punishments would result. There were some stories too about the science laboratories and the fiendish things that were kept in jars there and dangerous explosions that were the results of first years getting chemistry experiments wrong. Both Lisa and Amin were particularly looking forward to doing science at Woodtown and getting their hands on the Bunsen burners they had heard so much about, and so these tales made them a bit nervous.

Before the end of their final term at primary school, some teachers from Woodtown came over to Amin and Lisa's classes to talk to them about their new school. One of them was a science teacher and she said that all the stories they had heard were rubbish and that they would have a great time in science lessons, so they were not to be scared. Two weeks later Amin and Lisa met each other for the first time at a special induction day laid on at Woodtown for new entrants. Part of the day was a series of workshops in the science department. Lisa designed and made a rocket which she tested on the school field. It went over 200 feet (60 metres) into the air – she was so excited. Amin put his hand onto a sort of silver ball and all his hair stood on end when the teacher turned the machine on. He laughed when he saw the same thing happen to other children.

In the final week of term Amin and Lisa's teachers asked them if they would keep in touch by sending emails to let them know how they are getting on in their new school. Amin and Lisa both agreed that their teachers could share their emails with the new Y6 classes starting in September so that the children might not be worried about the move to the 'big school' when it was their turn later in the school year. Amin and Lisa's teachers said they would be particularly interested to know how they got on in science as that was the subject they were most excited about.

Here are a few of the emails that Amin and Lisa sent:

> From: lisa@woodtown.sch.uk
> Sent: 4th September
> To: Miss Coates
> Cc: Y6 at Blogtown Primary School
> Subject: My first week at Woodtown

Dear Miss Coates,

Settling in quite well. We had a big assembly which was a bit scary – so many others here and they are all so big! All the subjects so far are pretty cool. I had my first science lesson today and I have to cover my science exercise book and stick a copy of the lab rules into it for homework – so not so hard!

Miss you all – Lisa

> From: amin@woodtown.sch.uk
> Sent: 20th September
> To: Mr Wallace
> Cc: Y6 at Littleham Primary School
> Subject: Science at Woodtown

Dear Mr Wallace,

No problems here now – I am not scared anymore and we have all had older kids with us to help that are called our 'mentors'. Had a great science lesson today. We had to heat some water up with the Bunsen burner. I had to work with Lisa who is my practical partner. She had to tie her hair back. I wasn't scared of using the burner and Mr Benson was really nice to us. I feel like I'm doing science for real now.

Best wishes to all at Littleham

> From: lisa@woodtown.sch.uk
> Sent: 2nd October
> To: Miss Coates
> Cc: Y6 at Blogtown Primary School
> Subject: Science at Woodtown

Dear Miss Coates,

Today we did a lesson all about dissolving. We had a word bank on the wall and we had to use words like solution, dissolve, solute, suspension when we wrote up our practical. I knew most of the words from before at Blogtown and most of the others in the class did as well. It was a bit boring. At least we get to do the practical in pairs and not in groups of six or more.

Love Lisa

From: amin@woodtown.sch.uk
Sent: 27th October
To: Mr Wallace
Cc: Y6 at Littleham Primary School
Subject: Science

Dear Mr Wallace,

Today we had a plant and we had to draw it and name all the parts. Then we had to design an experiment to see what would be best to germinate some seeds. It was boring 'cos me and Lisa have both done the same at primary school.

Best wishes to all at Littleham

From: lisa@woodtown.sch.uk
Sent: 7th November
To: Miss Coates
Cc: Y6 at Blogtown Primary School
Subject: Science Test

Dear Miss Coates,

I still quite like science but some of the things are the same. We have had some hard new things to learn and we got a test about them. I got 50 out of 100 and I was a bit fed up as I couldn't see where I went wrong. It was good at primary school 'cos you used to talk to us about our work all the time but here we don't get that so much – we just have to go over the test.

Lisa

Amin and Lisa's story and their emails are of course fictitious. Their aspirations, fears and reactions, however, reflect fairly typical experiences. In composing them I drew on an idea used by Ian Morrison. He carried out a study in information and communication technology (ICT) lessons in which new entrants sent emails about their experiences of their new school to Y6 pupils in the primary schools they had attended the term before (Morrison, 2000). The purpose, as in Amin and Lisa's case, was to allay anxieties about the primary–secondary transfer among current and future cohorts of pupils in Y6 classes. It is an idea that others reading this may wish to replicate.

Science is at the top of most pupils' lists of subjects they look forward to in secondary school. As for Amin and Lisa, it is an exciting prospect, though one not without its fears. Pupils' voices and evaluations of schemes to address post-transfer 'settling in' show that over the past 15 years in the UK social aspects of transfer have been dealt with well and so most of the fears that pupils might have before and on arrival at their new schools are effectively addressed and soon disappear. This is testament to the great efforts made by many schools to improve primary–secondary transfer.

For many pupils, science in secondary schools now becomes more 'real'. You have a special place to do it (a laboratory), a special teacher, new things to use, and long, new technical words to learn. The new environment is enhanced by the theatricality of experience. The teacher (and sometimes the pupils) may wear a costume – a white coat. There are dramatic events sometimes spiced with a little danger. Induction days add to the hyping of secondary science – not that it needs much.

So, given all these advantages coupled with the natural curiosity in the world that children of this age show, why do Amin's and Lisa's emails show a waning enthusiasm for science after such a short time in their secondary school? While these are, of course, my constructions, narrative devices to promote thinking and debate about the issues, Amin's and Lisa's messages also contain some of the seeds of school science's demise. I will not discuss the reasons in detail here for there is far more to it than can be summarized in one story. In this book the voices of pupils and teachers and extensive surveys and evaluations of actions to improve primary–secondary transfer, particularly in science, are used to evidence progression and continuity in science learning, or rather the lack of it.

It is all very well knowing what the problems are, but most readers will also want to know what can be done to improve teaching and learning so that continuity is good and progression more assured. In many places in this book examples of activities, based on years of experience and research, are provided that can be adapted or used directly. Maintaining the good start with which primary science has often equipped pupils is vital in avoiding the disaffection with science that seems to be setting in at an earlier and earlier age in secondary schools. Worries about recruiting enough future scientists and in equipping the population with the types of scientific literacies and degrees of criticality needed to engage in modern society might seem a long way off for pupils aged 11, but attitudes formed at this age endure.

For too long it seems the education system, certainly in the UK, has been bedevilled by schisms and suspicions between what C.P. Snow (1993) called the 'two cultures', one dealing with the arts and humanities the other with the sciences. According to some, including Snow, for much of the twentieth century the petty jealousies and rivalries between subjects in the two 'cultures' dominated development and limited progress in education. George Smoot, the Nobel-winning astrophysicist who first identified the background radiation of the Big Bang and thereby effectiveley invented modern cosmology sees the 'two cultures' as an outmoded idea, irrelevant to the modern world. He claims we are entering a third culture now more heavily dominated by science and technology.

> Basically, in terms of whatever war (between the two cultures) has been going on, I think it has finished. I don't characterize it by saying we (the scientists) have won. I think everybody has won. We are living in a profound science culture and the big events that are affecting people's lives are scientific ones. (Smoot, quoted by Adams, 2007: 6)

There seems little doubt that Amin and Lisa's world will be increasingly dominated by these huge cultural shifts envisaged by Smoot. All of us in education have a vested interest in seeing more scientifically literate generations graduating from their periods of compulsory schooling. Ignorance of science, as in other fields of human endeavour, is a dangerous thing. We would be short-changing Amin and Lisa as human beings and compromising their futures as citizens if we did not recognize that. This book deals with starting points in this endeavour – a small yet crucial part of the effort.

Acknowledgements

I would like to acknowledge support of the AstraZeneca Science Teaching Trust in providing funds to support the projects at York to develop and evaluate bridging units in science. I would like to thank all the teachers who worked on the projects and agreed to be observed and interviewed, and pupils who took part in evaluation. Special thanks to Celia Moore who provided Chapter 5 and contributed to Chapter 9. It was inspirational to work with someone with such a wide range of experience in transfers and transitions, and who can see the 'bigger picture'.

Introduction

Points in our lives where we move from one phase to another have a significant impact. From childhood to adolescence, from being single to having a partner, changing jobs, retirement – often these are stressful times. Perhaps we have forgotten what it was like for us on that first morning in a new school, nervous in a new environment but expectant and excited too. Going to a new school is a 'rite of passage' in our early lives and, at transfer to secondary school, an entry into adulthood. As we learned from Amin and Lisa, science is one of the most exciting prospects about a new school. But their subsequent learning journeys, like countless others', are not as smooth as they might be. Part of the problem is work repeated without sufficient new interest and challenge for pupils and it is why the title of this book is phrased as a rhetorical question – *Starting Science ... Again?* This book is about helping the Amins and Lisas of this world make their way in a life enriched by, and increasingly dependent on, understanding science.

In 1985 the UK government was developing policy before introducing a 'national curriculum' that would define the content of subjects and how these were to be organised across the statutory age-range of schooling (5–16). During that process it was recognized that developing a science curriculum as a continuum demanded careful thought.

> The development of science in primary schools imposes an added responsibility on the schools to which the pupils transfer: they have to ensure, if the goal of making science from 5 to 16 a continuum is to be realized, that pupils' early start is neither ignored nor undervalued but rather reinforced and exploited in their subsequent work. Suitable arrangements for ensuring continuity and progression are therefore essential. (DES/WO, 1985: para. 32:11)

Perhaps it was a worry that teaching science in primary schools would be such a new development for many schools, which made government advisers cautious. So against this background the great national curriculum experiment came into being. With a spirally constructed, age-related design for learning (more of this in Chapter 1) came an expectation that teaching should be planned, especially at stages involving transfer from one school to another, to avoid needless repetition of work, and that would be capable of recognizing pupils' previous achievements and progressing these accordingly. But why was this seen as particularly important in science rather than in subjects such as mathematics, history or geography? It may have been that subject content, key ideas and skills in science, are seen as having to be progressively developed rather than compartmentalized into study of different periods as in history, regions as in geography or levels of numerical manipulation and abstraction as in mathematics. In these subjects it is easier to hive off different content to different programmes (and so ages) of study, though in reality I am sure progression in those subjects is much more complex than this. From the pupils' perspective things are a little simpler. In secondary school you are now studying the Tudors and not Romans and South America not England. But in science it is forces, energy, living things and materials – again. That this is natural because we have to progress learning of the 'big ideas' of science in a gradual way is lost on young minds ready and eager to learn new things. There are two ways of dealing with the problem. One is to adopt a *tabula rasa* approach where the teacher starts science as a new subject as if everything done before counted for nothing. Another, more fruitful approach, would be to find out what has been done before and design teaching that builds from those earlier experiences, no matter how naive and unsophisticated they might seem, persuading learners that knowing and understanding science requires careful, continual construction. Ruth Jarman, who led the way with her studies of primary–secondary transfer in science, sees secondary teachers as either *resumptionists*, most likely to repeat work because they doubt pupils' understanding or levels of competence, or as *recognitionists*, more likely to value previous learning and to collaborate with primary colleagues (Jarman, 1997). The aim of this book, then, is to increase the number of recognitionists and reduce the numbers of resumptionists.

A book about research *in* practice

In science education there has been a tendency to publish books for the researcher-scholar and a different set of books for the practitioner-teacher. This book is different. There are plenty of materials, activities and suggested actions for the practitioner-teacher to take directly 'off the shelf' or to adapt for their own situations. But I think doing just that would be a waste as it misses an understanding of how, when and why the recommended actions are likely to be most successful. Teaching, like medicine and law, is moving towards what is known as *evidence-based practice* (more of this in Chapter 10). Increasingly, trainee and practising teachers and managers are being asked to justify decisions on how to teach, and what resources support it, based on evidence of what works best. In this book I set out the strategies and methods used to improve progression and continuity in science against the research background used to design them and the outcomes as seen from perspectives of the main beneficiaries – pupils and teachers. As such it is a book that places research *in* the context of classroom pedagogy and pupil learning.

Schools are increasingly being asked to evaluate what they do and provide evidence to justify their choice of actions. It is important that teachers have effective tools to do this. *Starting Science … Again?* shares the methods of evaluation and background studies so that these can be used or adapted to help self-evaluation and action research.

Structure of the book

Each chapter begins with an overview of its content so that the reader has a clear idea of what it contains and the matters discussed. At the end of each chapter is a summary of the key points and suggestions for actions that teachers and others might want to consider. Where appropriate and useful there are questions to stimulate reflection and discussion. For those unfamiliar with the English National Curriculum or the school system in the UK, there is a glossary of important terms used in the book.

Chapter 1 concerns ways in which science learning is structured and the extent to which progression and continuity should have been assured by a national curriculum.

Chapter 2 presents evidence that after transfer to primary schools many pupils regress in science. The strategies used to address this post-transfer decline are reviewed.

Chapter 3 is concerned with pupils' views on the transition from primary to secondary school science. On the positive side pupils enjoy and look forward to science as a subject – particularly practical work – but they rarely see development of their skills as a continuous process.

In Chapter 4 we turn to the teachers' voices. It seems that secondary teachers do not trust the levels at which primary pupils have been assessed and accept that work, especially experiments, are often repeated. The implications of this are discussed.

In Chapter 5 Celia Moore reviews actions that schools can take to improve primary–secondary transfer. These include, open evenings, induction days and peer mentoring. Celia discusses the emotional needs of pupils and how administrative and other policies can make a huge difference to the progress of pupils after entry to secondary school.

Chapter 6 considers the use of bridging units to tackle discontinuities in teaching and disruptions in progression in science learning. The methods are evaluated so that teachers and others can get the most out of using this approach.

In Chapter 7 a more flexible approach to bridging the primary–secondary learning gap is considered. At the core of this approach is the need to make specific reference to pupils' previous work and what they will do next.

In Chapter 8 we consider the thorny issues of assessment and share some of the successful approaches developed in work at York.

In Chapter 9 we show how teachers can work together to better understand each others' approaches. Celia Moore adds case studies of interesting work in Wales and Suffolk that take co-teaching to new levels.

In the final Chapter 10 factors that drive policy on transfer and transition are considered, as are conditions under which many of the suggestions in this book might work best.

How to use this book

It would be possible to use this book very selectively. For example one could dive straight into Chapter 6 and read about how bridging units were designed and used and be aware of some of the pitfalls. Such a reader might then be better prepared to develop their own bridging programme. Those who want to know something about observing colleagues in an alternate phase of teaching could go directly to Chapter 9, or those interested in planning liaison meetings or induction visits could go to Celia Moore's chapter (5). The student teacher preparing for an essay on progression and continuity might go straight to Chapter 1 for background reading or the policy-maker wanting overall conclusions and ways forward to the final chapter. Of course, I hope there will be readers who want a more complete story of this complex and fascinating area. For them the book can and should be read as a whole.

The York-based science transfer projects

Much of the material in this book comes from two projects on primary–secondary transfer in science based at the University of York. Both projects were funded by the AstraZeneca Science Teaching Trust which provides support for professional and curriculum development in science education (www.azteachscience.co.uk). The projects involved pupils and teachers in over 80 primary schools and 16 high schools in three separate local authorities (LAs), the City of York, North Yorkshire and the East Riding of Yorkshire. From 2002 until 2007 a programme of training was offered to LA inspectors, senior managers, teachers and advisory teachers from schools, colleges and LA services interested in improving continuity and progression in science. Over 70 groups have been trained, and talks and workshops provided in 10 different countries.

The first project, the Science Transition AstraZeneca York (STAY) project involved a team of science educators and teachers from primary and secondary schools in research and development of a programme of teaching to be used either side of the primary–secondary transfer. Two 'bridging units', Fizzy Drinks and Bread, were subsequently taught and evaluated in schools in York and the East Riding. A second study called the North Yorkshire AstraZeneca Science Pedagogy and Progression (NYASPP) project involved a team of nine educators and expert teachers in development and evaluation of flexible approaches to transitions known as Scientific Enquiry Progression Tasks (SEPTs). Naturally, I have drawn heavily on this material.

1

Progression and Continuity in Learning Science

Chapter overview

Understanding progression and continuity in science learning is a prerequisite for thinking about how and why pupils do or do not move forward in their learning at transitions. Continuity and progression are considered in terms of conceptual and procedural knowledge and understanding of science. 'From → to' statements help the reader understand progression steps as they affect Key Stage 2 (KS2) and Key Stage 3 (KS3) pupils. The two areas of knowledge and understanding of science are linked by a model explaining continuity and progression in each and as part of a 'spiral' curriculum.

Continuity and progression are cornerstones of education, essential in understanding the construction of schooling in most countries. *Progression* describes pupils' personal journeys through education and ways in which they acquire, hone, apply and develop their skills, knowledge and understanding in increasingly challenging situations. *Continuity* is concerned with ways in which the education system structures experience and provides sufficient challenge and progress for pupils in a recognizable curricular landscape. The introduction of a national curriculum in the UK from 1989 was an opportunity to provide this landscape, with its spiral structure of age-related programmes of study, each providing assumed amounts of continuity and progression in demand through consistent and recognizable areas of experience (called 'attainment targets'). Unfortunately pupils' personal journeys through education are often more disjointed and discontinuous than this curriculum model assumes or can assure. There are major points of disjunction when pupils transfer from one programme of instruction to another, particularly when this transfer involves a change of school. How and why these disjunctions occur in learning science, and strategies that can be used to minimize if not eradicate these disjunctions and the setbacks in learning that result, are key subjects of this book. Before I consider where disjunctions commonly occur and why (in the next chapter), it is important to explore what the terms 'continuity' and 'progression' mean. This is fundamental to an understanding of transitions in learning science.

Continuity

I find landscape analogies useful when thinking about continuity. Thus continuity provides a safe and recognizable map for the personal journeys that individual learners make across it. Similarly, we can think of the subjects of the curriculum, history, geography, science, English, mathematics, and so on as recognizable landmarks, and the programmes of study and schemes of work as towns and villages, communities of knowledge and experiences if you like, to be visited each with optional routes between them. To extend my analogy to include progression, these journeys can be both forwards and backwards, uphill or downhill, thereby representing progression in moving forwards as well as the setbacks of regression. Explaining the ups and downs of progression/regression is an important point to which I return in the next chapter.

In working with primary student teachers at Bretton Hall College of the University of Leeds, my colleague Roy Phipps produced a summary of what he saw as the main points associated with continuity in learning science. I think this deals well with what we need to understand at this stage.

Continuity:

1 is about the nature of experiences pupils are offered
2 implies a consistency in aims, values and expectations
3 relies on good teacher–teacher relationships and communication
4 should require teachers and schools receiving pupils from another class or key stage to give attention to the learning children have already received
5 is facilitated in the UK National Curriculum through programmes of study carrying similar titles across all key stages and through a common language and scheme for assessment (see the Glossary for definitions of National Curriculum terms).

These tenets associated with the concept of continuity sound very fine and are certainly in sympathy with the intentions of the National Curriculum as it existed in the early 1990s, but we will see throughout this book that many of them are much less assured, in pupils' experience, than we might assume.

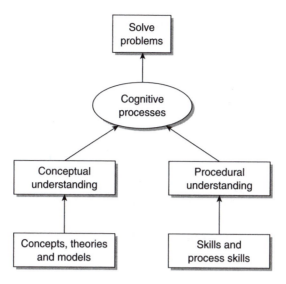

Figure 1.1   A model for school science (based on Gott and Duggan, 1995: 25)

Progression in learning science

In considering progression in science learning, I think it is important to look at two interrelated areas: *procedural* and *conceptual* understanding. This idea derives from a model proposed for learning science where *cognitive processes* required to solve problems, whether they be purely practical or about reaching new levels of understanding ideas about the world, draw on two distinct but interacting sets of knowledge, both of which have to be taught (Gott and Duggan, 1995) (see Figure 1.1). *Conceptual understanding* requires learners to draw on the known facts, laws and theories of science, and models that have been devised to help explain these, to reach progressively more sophisticated levels of understanding of how the world works. *Procedural understanding* requires 'thinking behind the doing' (Gott and Dugan, 1995: 26). In this way science, like any other subject, has a set of unique procedures that come into play, for example, when planning and designing tests of the reliability and validity of evidence to support an idea or hypothesis, and deciding what measurements are needed to collect data. Other procedural knowledge is drawn upon to decide how best to represent data and what patterns or new ideas emerge from analysis. The National Curriculum was constructed with progression in both of these areas of knowledge and understanding in mind, though the chopping and changing of documentation from one version of the curriculum to the next over the past 20 years has meant that the progression lines are often hard to see. An aim of this chapter is to clarify these lines of progression.

Progression in conceptual understanding

The spiral curriculum

Most commentators on the evolution of the school curriculum and its design acknowledge the influence of Jerome Bruner (b. 1915). Bruner realized that construction of knowledge relies on a continual process through which learners develop complexity of thinking by integrating new experiences, observations and knowledge with what they already know and have experienced. According to Bruner the child already possesses some sort of mental templates for interpreting the world, new experiences are matched against these and, eventually, the templates develop and change to accommodate new ways of thinking about the world (Bruner, 1966).

In his classic text, *The Process of Education*, Bruner proposed a 'spiral curriculum' through which to accommodate, 'the great issues and values that society deems worthy of the continual concern of its members' (Bruner, 1960: 2). Bruner described the principle behind the spiral curriculum in the following way:

> I was struck by the fact that successful efforts to teach highly structured bodies of knowledge like mathematics, physical science and even the field of history often took the form of a metaphoric spiral in which at some simple level a set of ideas or operations are introduced in a rather intuitive way and, once mastered in that spirit, were then revisited and reconstructed in a more formal or operational way, then being connected with other knowledge, the mastery at this stage then being carried one step higher to a new level of formal or operational rigour and to a broader level of abstraction and comprehensiveness. The end stage of this process was the eventual mastery of the connectivity and structure of a large body of knowledge ... (Bruner, 1960: 3–4)

We can see from this that Bruner drew heavily on the idea of developmental stages identified by Jean Piaget (see Gardner, 2001). For Bruner it was not only a question of what intellectual capacities already existed in the minds of children at different developmental stages but also how step-by-step changes in the abilities to interpret and rethink information and experiences are used. In this way Bruner was thinking about the *cognitive structures* that might develop through revisiting areas of experience and knowledge, and how children might lay on new layers of knowledge and new interpretations to develop their thinking about phenomena and concepts met before. In science learning, this 'layering' process of thinking resonates with many examples taught in the school curriculum. Table 1.1 is one illustration of this.

The progression in the explanations provided in Table 1.1 seems logical to us (as adults and teachers) and so might seem relatively unproblematic to teach. But this is because we are seeing through the lens of adulthood and from our informed vantage point at the top of the 'layered learning cake'. I have often found that, for the child, explanations can seem counterintuitive and odd, often clashing with naive (but to the child much more logical and useful) reasoning. For example, it is often more obvious to a child

Table 1.1 'Layers' of thinking about evaporation (of a puddle)

Observations and explanations	'Layer' of thinking
Puddles disappear	Basic experience of a phenomenon
Puddles disappear faster when it is windy	Link between cause and effect
When puddles disappear the water evaporates	Early conceptual thinking
Puddles disappear faster when it is windy because the air above them does not get saturated with water vapour	Conceptual development linking cause and effect
Washing on a line also dries faster on a windy day for the same reason	Application of the concept to provide explanations for other phenomena (generalization)

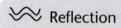 Reflection

Try drawing up tables showing progression for concepts associated with other phenomena, such as switching on an electric light or an apple decaying.

that water in a puddle merely soaks away into the ground rather than parts of it (molecules that are invisible) leaving the surface to enter air. Thus, linking cause and effect requires rationalization based on evidence that challenges existing ideas and moves thinking on. The mental effort of doing this is significant. This is where the skill of the teacher comes in. In my own teaching for example, I found that those naive, intuitive ideas could be challenged by evaporating bowls of water, some with impermeable plastic bases and some covered by clear plastic so trapping re-condensed vapour as liquid water. Research, however, indicates that such one-off experiences are often not enough to permanently shift thinking to new levels (Driver et al., 1985; Osborne and Freyburg, 1985). I see learning science like a slowly constructed jigsaw. In some lessons and through some experiences more of the pieces fall into place; at worst some pieces already there are lost or do not seem to fit the picture anymore. The teacher's job is to draw on her or his tool kit of experience and knowledge about children and teaching to decide what experiences and learning tools are most likely to move thinking in more fruitful directions. Some call this crucial professional knowledge – pedagogical content knowledge (PCK) – and providing or enhancing it is effectively the basis of much that we do in initial teacher training (ITT) and continuing professional development (CPD) of teachers.

Steps and leaps in understanding

In a very useful handbook for science teachers published by the Association for Science Education (ASE), Asoko and Squires (1998: 178) refer to different amounts of *cognitive effort* required by pupils to reach new layers of understanding.

Modest leaps in understanding   These require relatively small steps linking experience and new knowledge, and extending it in limited ways. For example, experience that some metals conduct electricity and others do not could be extended by showing that electricity is conducted to different extents in the metals that do conduct. When studying the distribution of plants on a field, pupils might learn that different areas contain different collections of plants. This experience could be extended to discover that occurrence and distribution of plants might be linked to an environmental factor such as the amount of water available or a human factor such as the amount of trampling by feet.

Major leaps in understanding   These require a shift from observation and description of phenomena and simple linking of cause and effect to explanations requiring more abstract thinking, often through the application of advanced ideas or conceptual models. For example, the layer of thinking requiring an explanation of rates of evaporation in terms of the relative saturation of air with water, referred to in Table 1.1, requires thinking about evaporation in terms of a model of particles and how they are arranged and move. The teacher's PCK here relies on judging how much abstraction from the model is needed to help pupils shift their ideas without them losing contact with the explanations that have been perfectly satisfactory (and of value to them) so far.

Constructing frameworks of understanding   These are sometimes referred to as the 'big ideas' or 'key ideas' of science (Millar et al., 2001). There are frameworks, ways of thinking, that have helped scientists make sense of concepts, models and theories and can be applied in several contexts and across different scientific disciplines. For example the framework of thinking called 'energy' unifies ideas about what forms energy takes and what happens to it as it is transferred around various systems. The framework holds equally true for, and is helpful in understanding, what happens in physical systems such as heat transfer, in chemical reactions and for studying 'flows' of energy in ecosystems. These frameworks are what Bruner envisaged when he wrote about 'broader levels of abstraction and comprehensiveness' and the 'connectivity and structure of a larger body of knowledge' (Bruner, 1960: 3–4). Part of the teachers' PCK required here is to realize the value of consistency and unity of language in teaching. One issue in teaching about energy ideas in secondary schools has been that teachers, often in separate and distinct departments dealing with biology, physics and chemistry, have used the supposedly unifying framework of 'energy' inconsistently. The same terms or ideas are used to mean quite different things in different lessons. This was something that a move to integrated or combined science teaching in the 1980s was supposed to have addressed. For example in one scheme, Suffolk Coordinated Science, it was recommended that 'a common language and use of conceptual models should be used by teachers from all disciplines when teaching about energy' (Dobson, 1987: 90–7). Dobson even set out how the framework of ideas should be developed and progressed across the age range taught (1987: 14–16).

From → to statements

In an effort to address some of the complexities of conceptual progression discussed, research and development teams at York felt that teachers would benefit from seeing progression in terms of statements showing clear lines of development (NCC, 1991; Qualter et al., 1990). These so-called 'from → to' statements had previously been prominent in guidance connected with the development of procedural knowledge (knowledge associated with practical science) associated with an attainment target devoted to the 'Exploration of Science'. This attainment target was considered at the time it was introduced in 1989 to represent a different and more open-ended model of practical science than had previously been taught and thus outside the experience of most practising teachers. By the late 1990s, guidance associated with the introduction of a national curriculum for initial teacher training combined some of these statements about procedural knowledge with others on conceptual development (DfEE and TTA, 1998a; 1998b). I have provided some of this in Text Box 1.1 as I think it summarizes quite well some of the most important aspects of progression in school science.

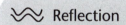 Reflection

The examples of progression shown in Text Box 1.1 could be mapped against schemes of work to see how they are accounted for. This might be a useful activity for student teachers.

Progression in the 'process skills' of science

What are process skills?

Procedural understanding, as conceived in Gott and Duggan's model (see Figure 1.1), deals with learning of what Harlen has called *process skills* (Harlen, 1997). It is important to understand what we mean by 'process skills' as these will be referred to throughout this book. Science educators often use the terms 'skills' and 'processes' to define important aspects that can be recognized when pupils carry out practical work in science, but the terms are often confused. So what is the difference between *skills* and *processes*?

Text Box 1.1

Progression considered at primary school level (adapted from Teacher Training Agency, 2000a)

- **from** using everyday language **to** an increasingly precise use of technical and scientific vocabulary, notation and symbols
- **from** personal scientific knowledge in a few areas **to** understanding in a wider range of areas and of links between areas
- **from** describing events and phenomena **to** explaining events and phenomena
- **from** explaining phenomena in terms of their own ideas **to** explaining phenomena in terms of accepted scientific ideas or models
- **from** participating in practical science activities **to** building increasingly abstract models of real situations
- **from** unstructured exploration **to** more systematic investigation of a question
- **from** using simple drawings, diagrams and charts to represent and communicate scientific information **to** using more conventional diagrams and graphs.

Progression considered at secondary school level (adapted from Teacher Training Agency, 2000b)

- **from** understanding of accepted scientific knowledge in a few areas **to** understanding in a wide range of areas including, where relevant, the links between areas
- **from** describing events and simple phenomena **to** explaining events and more complex phenomena
- **from** explaining phenomena in terms of their own ideas **to** explaining phenomena in terms of accepted scientific ideas or models
- **from** a study of observable phenomena **to** increasing use of formal and generalized ideas
- **from** an essentially qualitative view of phenomena **to**, where appropriate, a more quantitative and mathematical view
- **from** seeing science as a school activity **to** an understanding of the nature and impact of scientific and technological activity beyond the classroom
- **from** experiment and investigation involving simple scientific ideas **to** those in which

    - more complex scientific ideas may be drawn upon
    - more than one variable may be pertinent
    - decisions have to be made about strategies and instruments for data collection
    - data is interpreted and evaluated in terms of strengths and limitations

(Continued)

(Continued)

- **from** accepting models and theories uncritically **to** recognizing how new evidence may require modifications to be made
- **from** simple drawings, diagrams and charts representing scientific information or data **to** diagrams and graphs which use scientific conventions
- **from** using a limited range of scientific language, notation and symbols **to** using an extended technical vocabulary and standard notation and symbols routinely, appropriately and correctly.

Skills   describe small-scale or short-term actions, decisions or routines that underpin practical work.

Processes   are sets of procedures that deal with the *thinking* and *decision-making* about how to deploy skills. In this way processes link to what are sometimes described as 'thinking skills'.

Carrying out a *process* while doing practical work relies on knowing and being able to deploy a number of *skills*. For example if you ask a pupil to find the warmest location in the classroom this involves the *process* of measurement which requires the pupil to think about *what* to measure, *where* to measure and *how* to measure. In carrying out the measurement of temperature, a number of *skills* are used: choosing a thermometer with an appropriate range for the task, manipulating the thermometer in a way that will provide an accurate measure and then taking a reading against the instrument's scale. For most of the time in this book we can say that 'process skills' are broadly equivalent to 'processes'.

In the training associated with the development of bridging work in the STAY project we found that having a list of 'process skills' was useful because it helped teachers focus on the elements of practical work that are essential to a particular (transition) task in hand. This helps in planning, that is, deciding what your objectives for practical work are, and in assessing, that is, deciding how you will judge pupil outcomes in relation to specific process skills rather than trying to assess many different outcomes at the same time.

The *process skills* of scientific enquiry are:

- Raising questions
- Planning
- Predicting
- Measuring
- Observing
- Recording and communicating
- Interpreting evidence
- Drawing conclusions
- Explaining
- Evaluating evidence
  (adapted from Harlen, 1996; Harlen and Jelly, 1996).

In a project developing partnership teaching in primary schools (funded by the AZSTT) in Barnsley, Wakefield and York, I found that understanding process skills helped teachers disentangle what pupils were doing in science practical work and to plan more effectively to develop particular, targeted process skills (Crebbin, 2001). Teachers told me that they found teaching practical work (Attainment Target 1 of the National Curriculum) difficult because they assumed pupils should be involved in most if not all process skills in one practical lesson so making it hard for them to identify pupils' problems and provide appropriate support. In many ways this was a case of seeing the process skills *wood* through the *forest* of scientific enquiry. I think that one of the reasons there has been so much confusion about what is to be taught and how it is to be assessed is because of the many changes in emphasis in Attainment Target 1 in the four revisions of the National Curriculum for science between its inception in 1989 and the version in use today (Braund, 1996). So, sorting out what is the real progression in process skills seemed a necessary step forward in any work on transitions.

Process skills are fundamental in developing understanding of phenomena and concepts and in testing out theory as Gott and Duggan's model (Figure 1.1) implies. For example, the ability to consider and question evidence is vital if pupils are to accept or disregard conflicting ideas. This is essential in helping pupils develop new understanding by moving away from naive assumptions, for example, about dissolving, to a more sophisticated understanding of what is involved.

In the past it was often assumed that process skills would be learned integrally, that is, that merely carrying out practical tasks was enough for pupils to develop an understanding and that further practice would embed skills and hone performance. Current thinking is that, just as with the rest of science, *process skills have to be taught.* The AKSIS (ASE and Kings College Science Investigations in Schools) materials contain resources that help teachers develop pupils' process skills through direct teaching (see, for example, Goldsworthy, et al., 2000; Watson and Wood Robinson, 1998). The aim of these materials is to encourage specific teaching of process skills rather than allow pupils to discover how to improve on these through the often busy and less structured learning environment of open-ended practical work.

Mapping progression in science process skills

The first version of the National Curriculum for science (DES/WO, 1989) included an entire attainment target ('Exploration of Science') devoted to development of procedural understanding, though that phrase was not used at the time. The mere existence of any part associated with practical science, especially one carrying a weighting in teaching and testing of 50 per cent at Key Stage 1 and 40 per cent at Key Stage 2, was a triumph in the face of adversity. At the time I was working for the Assessment of Performance Unit at the University of Leeds and I know that members of Her Majesty's Inspectorate

(HMI) involved in negotiations on the National Curriculum came under enormous pressure to slim down the overambitious document produced by the Science Working Group (SWG) in 1988 (DES/WO, 1988b). The SWG recommended 22 attainment target areas in the programmes of study, five of which referred to practical experience (Braund, 1996; Graham, 1993). Fearing that practical experience might be lost from the National Curriculum altogether, HMI turned to the researchers from the Assessment of Performance Unit (APU) in Science based at Kings College London and the University of Leeds who had researched performance in most of the process skills identified by Harlen at ages 11, 13 and 15 over a period of 10 years (Archenhold, 1988; Russell, 1998; Schofield, 1989). Thus what appeared in the 1989 programmes of study, and especially in criteria for assessing outcomes of practical work at least had some sound foundation in research (DES/WO, 1989). In my view these assessment criteria represented the clearest progression for investigative work that the National Curriculum has ever contained. The need to slim down weighty and unworkable documentation during the 1990s meant that at each revision these progression lines became less distinct.

To fill the gap in guidance on progression in process skills in Attainment Target 1 and provide something more useful for teachers in planning for progression, the project team at York working on the second of the science transition projects (the North Yorkshire AstraZeneca Science Pedagogy and Progression [NYASPP] project) devised sets of from → to statements for most of the process skills identified by Harlen (1997). These are provided as Text Box 1.2. While I do not claim these statements are a full picture of progression routes within each process skill across the age range of the National Curriculum, I think they do provide an important guide relevant to the KS2 → KS3 transfer discussed in this book.

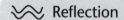 Reflection

Compare pairs of practical activities used in similar content areas either side of the KS2/3 transfer to see if progression in relevant process skills is in line with that recommended in Text Box 1.2.

Another device we have used to help teachers understand progression in procedural understanding in specific process skills is to provide extracts from pupils' work and to order these as progression from least to most developed. In training associated with transition projects at York we used this to look at progression in one key area of Attainment Target 1, *considering and evaluating evidence*. This area was chosen as it received increased emphasis in the 2000 revision of the National Curriculum for science and had received much less attention in teaching compared with aspects such as 'fair testing' and planning of investigations (Goldsworthy et al., 2000). To help think about progression in this area we identified five sub-themes:

Text Box 1.2

From → to statements for seven of the process skills identified by Harlen (1996)

Observation

Describing objects, phenomena and events in some detail. → Justifying why, and saying how, observations are made.

Understanding that human senses sometimes need assistance. → Choosing appropriate aids to make observations.

Making repeated observations to check results. → Linking quality and quantity of observations to 'concepts of evidence'.

Measurement

Measurements of basic quantities (mass, length, time, volume, temperature). → Repeated and accurate measures of basic *and* derived quantities (for example, velocity/rate).

Choosing equipment suitable for the type of measure to be made. → Choosing the appropriate measuring range of a piece of equipment.

Reading major scale divisions. → Reading minor scale divisions.

Predicting

Making a statement of expectation based on limited scientific reasoning. → Justifying predictions in terms of science ideas.

Giving some idea of the sequence, order or magnitude of events or effects. → Using evidence to give reasoned predictions of the sequence, order or magnitude of events or effects.

Planning

Identifying some effect factors and realizing that one has to be changed while others are controlled. → Identifying most of the key factors that might have an effect. Selecting factors to control.

Recording and communicating (graphs)

Realizing when line graphs and bar graphs should be used. → Constructing line graphs.

Constructing graphs with some help.

Beginning to decide on axes and scales for graphs. → Choosing appropriate axes and scales for graphs.

(Continued)

(Continued)

Interpreting evidence

Recognizing simple trends and patterns in results. ⟶ Describing detailed patterns in results, for example, changes over time.

Evaluating evidence

Knowing when some results don't fit the pattern and beginning to wonder why. ⟶ Identifying and explaining anomalous results.

Realizing that single results might not occur again. ⟶ Linking reliability of findings to the spread of readings.

Beginning to reflect on experimental design. ⟶ Linking reliability to experimental design where appropriate.

Source: Braund et al., 2004: 2–3

1 Seeking patterns and describing relationships in results.
2 Identifying and explaining anomalous results.
3 Appreciating and explaining the degree of reliability in findings.
4 Relating predictions to outcomes and suggesting scope for further enquiry.
5 Explaining findings in terms of existing or developing scientific knowledge and understanding.

The mixed-up pupils' responses for sub-themes relate to a specific investigation, the effect on bubble-blowing of mixing varying amounts of bubble mixture and glycerine. An example of one of these mixed-up, response sort activities, for the sub-theme, 'seeking patterns and describing relationships', is provided in Text Box 1.3.

In this activity sophisticated responses describe the relationship between the length of time bubbles last and the amount of glycerine in the mixture. The order of increasing progression from undeveloped reasoning to the most sophisticated response is 2 → 1 → 3 → 5 → 4. Response 4 is the most precise and developed one because it identifies that the bubbles last longer as the amount of glycerine is increased but only up to a certain point. Beyond this the length of time bubbles last actually decreases. Responses can be given out as cards but printing them onto acetate sheets, and cutting up the statements so they are separated, makes it easier for groups to feedback their views of progression. Participants place pieces of acetate in their chosen order onto a blank overhead projector transparency and write notes alongside these showing reasoning behind their choices. An interactive whiteboard could be used to achieve the same outcome. The activity has been used successfully with a variety of participants including teachers, advisers, consultants and student teachers.

Text Box 1.3

Mixed-up statements for the sub-theme of considering and evaluating evidence, 'Seeking patterns and describing relationships in results'

> 1
> The results show it was best when we added some glycerine to the bubble mixture.

> 2
> When we added glycerine the results were different to the results with just the bubble mixture on its own.

> 3
> The bubbles became better and better as we added more and more glycerine to the bubble mixture.

> 4
> With more glycerine in the bubble mixture the bubbles lasted longer – until we got to 2.5 cm^3. After that the bubble didn't last as long.

Source: Braund and Driver, 2005b, unit 5: 1–6

Integrating progression in procedural and conceptual understanding in science

In this chapter I have put forward the idea that progression in science learning can be viewed in two dimensions, one associated with the learning and understanding of concepts and the other with procedural understanding required to solve problems through practical activity. There is a danger, however, in assuming these are distinct areas of knowledge separated in teaching. It is my view that to divorce practical experience from the concepts it is designed to illuminate is a dangerous fallacy. The notion of concept-free practical activity has little credibility. In the 1980s a number of teaching schemes such as Science in Process (ILEA, 1987) and Warwick Process Based Science (Screen, 1986) promoted science teaching in the early years of secondary school that purported to be concerned mainly with development and application of 'processes' rather than advancing knowledge and understanding of science. Indeed, the second of these schemes treated processes as if they could be taught in a hierarchical way, observation followed by measurement, followed by prediction, followed by planning investigations, hypothesizing and so on. This led to a division among science educators, some of whom argued that hiving off process from content was dangerously artificial and others who claimed it was a perfectly valid way of introducing the study of science and more engaging for pupils. This so called 'processes versus content' debate culminated in a series of critiques of the process-led approach that also began to re-examine the very purposes of science education (see, for example, Hodson, 1988; Millar and Driver, 1987).

While it is beyond the scope of this chapter, and probably a distraction for me to go further into the debate on processes versus concepts, it is worth considering one attempt to integrate the two areas of scientific knowledge and so to provide a view of how this fits Bruner's notion of the spiral curriculum. In 1990 my APU colleagues based at Kings College, London, put together a book about progression in science explorations, drawing from over a decade of APU's large-scale research (Qualter et al., 1990). In this book a model was proposed showing the relationship between procedural knowledge (which they called 'Exploration of Science') and conceptual knowledge (which they called 'Knowledge and Understanding'). This model is provided as Figure 1.2.

In Qualter et al.'s model the solid and dotted lines represent the two areas of learning science as four turns of a double spiral; each turn representing one of the key stages of the National Curriculum. Thus the double spiral model reminds us that procedures and concepts are revisited in each key stage. The two parallel spirals are linked by 'blobs' representing investigations (today we might call these 'practical experiences'). Each 'experiential blob' has associated letters 'p' and 'c', alluding to the fact that the level of the concept underpinning each investigation and the procedures necessary to carry it out progress in terms of demand and complexity in line with the content of the programmes of study for each key stage (Qualter et al., 1990: 48). My APU colleagues drew on research work showing progression in the demand and complexity of scientific investigations and added this to the x and y axes of their model. As in Gott and Duggan's approach, the model reminds us that scientific investigations and, more broadly, practical experiences provide a matrix or 'glue' that helps pupils to make sense of scientific ideas and to test the robustness of the theories and evidence on which they are based. In modern National Curriculum parlance this provides an essential part of authenticating scientific activity as part of what is now called 'how science works'.

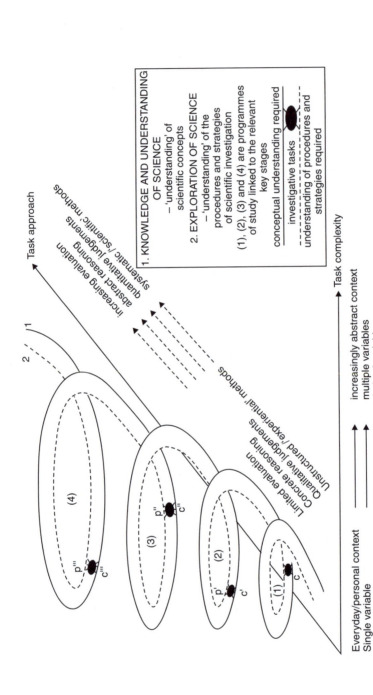

Figure 1.2 An integrated model of progression in science

Source: (Qualter et al., 1990: 49)

Summary

In this chapter the importance of continuity and progression in a spiral curriculum model providing pupils with opportunities to build competence in procedural understanding to develop and refine understanding of scientific concepts has been discussed. Successive revisions of the National Curriculum have made progression lines in procedural understanding less clear and so methods to improve on this have been included. *Conceptual* and *procedural* areas of science combine to help pupils build progressively new levels of thinking.

Suggested actions

- Use from → to statements to clarify progression lines when planning schemes of work and sequences of lessons, and in liaison meetings with teachers in alternate key stages.
- Try using mixed-up statements of pupils' work to help others clarify lines of progression in procedural or conceptual understanding.

2

Moving up – but Why Don't They Always Move on?

Chapter overview

Key moments of transition and transfer in education are listed. Evidence for post-transfer regression from national test results in England is shown and critiqued. The explanations for this regression and why it is particularly bad in science are reviewed from the teacher's perspective and from what research has to say. Results of school surveys show changing emphases on actions to address post-transfer regression.

As in life generally so it is in education. In life we go through moments of transition that sometimes result in disruption and maybe, even, relative dysfunction. Growing up and physiological changes associated with puberty and later the menopause are things we cannot determine. Marriage, divorce, moving house or changing job are humanly determined. All mark significant transitional moments in our lives some of which mean setbacks as well as points from which we travel forwards. The educational life of the child is a relatively long one. Yet from the child's point of view it is most of life at the time it is experienced. That the Key Stage 2 → Key Stage 3 (KS2/3) transfer coincides with the dramatic changes of puberty adds an extra dimension.

First let us remind ourselves of some of the key moments of educational transition. Maurice Galton, perhaps the leading expert on primary–secondary transfer in the UK, defines the points where learning, as experienced by pupils, goes through significant change or disruption as *transitions*. Where these transitions coincide with more major change, for example, of school, he calls these points *transfers* (Galton et al., 1999). Key transition points, some of which also involve transfer, are listed below.

- From pre-schooling (for example, kindergarten or nursery) → formal schooling, Key Stage 1 (may involve transfer).
- From Key Stage 1 → Key Stage 2 (may involve transfer).
- From Key Stage 2 → Key Stage 3 (nearly always involves transfer).
- From Key Stage 3 → Key Stage 4 (involves transfer in some middle school systems).
- From Key Stage 4 (GCSE) → sixth form or to work-based training (can involve transfer, for example, to a college).
- From sixth form to university or college or to work (always involves transfer).

For readers not accustomed to the ages of key stages of the UK National Curriculum, and other terms, these are defined in a Glossary at the end of the book.

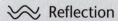 Reflection

> Before reading on, select one transition point and list aspects that might cause disruptions for pupils learning science. Discuss with colleagues what might cause these disruptions. Your discussions can be compared with what others have said – see Table 2.2.

There are also more minor points of transition: from one year to another within a key stage, from one topic to the next and, at the smallest scale, from one activity to another within lessons. All can impact on pupils' learning, sometimes in negative ways. For example, a change of teacher from one year to another or from one topic to another might mean pupils having to adjust to new behavioural codes and ways of working. The job of school policy and departmental planning is to put in place programmes and policies that recognize the important progression steps in what is to be learned but which minimize the disruption in learning that these transitions might cause. For example, schools might adopt common policies on behaviour management and codes of conduct that must be applied equally and consistently through all years of the school, or there might be agreement on progression lines and the key words to be introduced or developed across different topics. These ideas are developed more fully by Celia Moore in Chapter 5.

Progression or regression?

If the theory and rhetoric of progression and the spiral curriculum model discussed in the previous chapter worked out in practice and teachers heeded the

Table 2.1 Pupils achieving target levels in national curriculum tests at the end of Key Stage 2 (age 11) and end of Key Stage 3 (age 14)

	Percentage of pupils at or above target level in end of Key Stage 2 tests				Percentage of pupils at or above target level in end of Key Stage 3 tests		
	English	Mathematics	Science		English	Mathematics	Science
2000	75	72	85	2003	68	70	68
2001	75	71	87	2004	68	70	68
2002	75	71	86	2005	74	74	70
2003	75	73	87	2006	73	77	72
2004	78	74	86	2007	74	76	73

Source: data extracted from the National Statistics Database at www.statistics.gov. uk/STATBASE/Product.asp?vlnk=14679

progression lines enshrined in the programmes of study and associated assessment schemes, then we could assume that disjunctions represented by transitions and associated transfers of schools would not last very long – the impact on progression as evidenced by pupils' advances in performance would be small. We might expect, therefore, that a comparison of pupils' performance on national tests taken at the end of Key Stage 2 (age 11) and at the end of Key Stage 3 (age 14) should show an advance (or at least consistency) in the numbers who achieve the target level for the specified age group – in other words, that there are signs of progression. The figures in Table 2.1 (for tests in England) show this is clearly *not* the case, especially for science.

Previous comparisons have reported national test results for the two key stages for calendar years, but this is invalid as data are drawn from different populations of pupils. In Table 2.1 I have therefore compared the percentages of pupils who achieved the expected target level at the end of Key Stage 2 (level 4 or above) with the percentages of the *same population* of pupils three years later at the end of Key Stage 3. At the end of Key Stage 3 the expected target level is level 5 or above. What the figures show is that at worst nearly a third of pupils who were at or above the target level for science at age 11 failed to make the progress, by the end of Key Stage 3, that their performance predicted they should have. In English and mathematics the same pupils do not show anything like as severe a regression in performance. Indeed, in recent years (from 2004) there are signs that in English and mathematics the 'regression gap' has closed and more pupils are now achieving the KS3 target than did so in KS2, while science remains in negative regression mode. This pattern in test results when first noticed in the late 1990s was widely reported to government (see, for example, Galton's first review for the DfES [Galton et al., 1999]) and was one of the main reasons why the government invested nearly £1 billion in a national strategy to improve teaching at Key Stage 3 (initially known as the Key Stage 3 Strategy and later as the Secondary Strategy).

There have been claims that these comparisons of test results give a false picture mainly because tests in science cannot be compared robustly with those in mathematics and English. Chief among these criticisms is that science tests at Key Stage 2 are merely a memory test of certain facts and terms and that intensive revision periods before tests inflate performance levels – in other words, test results represent insubstantial, surface and ephemeral knowledge that soon dissipates after pupils transfer to secondary schools. A further criticism is that tests at Key Stage 3 are based on a programme of study that draws on much more demanding and abstract concepts requiring more than the simple descriptions and basic pattern recognition required at Key Stage 2. On the other hand, we must remember that tests have changed radically at both key stages since 2002 and now include a significant proportion of questions (about 40 per cent at each key stage) that require application of procedural knowledge and understanding such as about variables for investigation, recognition of patterns and relationships, strategies for measurement and interpretation of graphs and tables. It could be argued that procedural understanding should be more substantial, less ephemeral and less prone to inflation through revision.

Although there has been a slight closing of the regression gap in science since 2002, the basic trend and the negative comparisons with performances in English and mathematics continue. One could also claim that similar conceptual leaps from one stage to another exist in mathematics and yet the same populations of pupils do not show as much regression, and indeed since 2004 there is evidence of distinct advance in numbers in the subject who reach the KS3 target compared with numbers who reached the KS2 target. Additional, and perhaps stronger, evidence challenging the critique comes from retests administered in secondary schools using the same questions from national test papers taken at the end of the primary phase. These have shown similar or even greater amounts of regression to those seen in comparisons of national test results (Braund, 2007; Nicholls and Gardner, 1999; Bunyan, 1998). Findings from this research are used in more detail in later chapters to inform the design and use of strategies to improve KS2/3 progression in science.

Before I move on to explaining this post-transfer regression, it is worth examining one other piece of research comparing primary and secondary science. In 1976 Galton described teaching and learning in classrooms in primary, middle (with ages 9–13, see Glossary) and secondary schools, the ORACLE project (Observational Research and Classroom Learning Evaluation; Galton et al., 1980). Twenty years on, the ORACLE research was repeated and lessons in English, mathematics and science were observed in primary schools, the same pupils being seen again some months after they had transferred to their secondary schools. Galton's research team measured pupils' on-task behaviour in lessons, allocating pupils to different 'pupil personae' (Hargreaves and Galton, 2002). They found that the numbers of pupils showing high levels of on-task behaviour declined in science following transfer. In mathematics and English, on-task behaviour actually increased slightly. Since these pupils did not show dislike for science before or after transfer, the researchers explained their findings in terms of a probable boredom factor, perhaps connected with repetition of work covered before in primary school or a perception that activities were just uninteresting compared with previous teaching in primary schools.

Explaining post-transfer regression in science

Post-transfer regression: what the teachers say

Transition project and research teams at York held over 50 CPD and training events, conference presentations and workshops for teachers, student teachers, advisers and others. At 20 of these training events participants were asked to list what they thought were the most important explanations for regression in science (dip in pupils' performance and learning) at various transition/transfer points. Table 2.2 summarizes the most common explanations provided. It is worth noting that no new reasons were added after the first three workshops held, and this can be taken to show that these are probably the most important explanations as far as many science educators are concerned. An interesting observation is that most of the explanations for post-transfer regression in science at the KS2/3 transfer are the same as those for the Key Stage 4 → sixth form transfer.

One comment about transition from KS3 to KS4 is particularly revealing. It seems that some teachers recognized positive benefits of the Key Stage 3 Strategy for Science but seemed to think that the efforts to improve and enliven teaching and learning were not so readily or easily applied at KS4 where GCSE specifications tend to determine what is taught and learned. The intention of the Secondary Strategy, in place since 2004, is to extend successes of the KS3 strategy upwards to influence teaching in GCSE classes. However, recent criticisms of science teaching at this older age range continue, claiming, for example, that much science teaching is still 'boring' and reliant on a narrow range of pedagogical skills and so does not engage learners (House of Lords, 2006).

Responses in Table 2.2 and a number of research surveys suggest that explanations for post-transfer decline (overall), and why this should be worse in science (specifically), fall into two broad categories: social factors and pedagogic or curriculum effects. The social impacts of primary–secondary transfer are well known and are among the first to come to mind when teachers are asked to provide explanations. Research studies confirm that a new, larger and more challenging environment, new friendship groupings, more teachers and new rules all make demands on incoming pupils (Braund et al., 2003; Galton et al., 1999; Lee et al., 1995; Schagen and Kerr, 1999). The experience of many teachers in England, however, seems to be that with good pastoral care and efficient management of the transfer process, the social impact of these changes can quickly be ameliorated so that pupils settle into their new environment. Surveys confirm this is where most effort on transitions and transfers has been

Table 2.2 Explaining post-transfer pupil 'regression' in science

From KS2 → KS3	From KS3 → KS4	From KS4 → sixth form study	From AS → A2
Teaching styles in secondary classes differ from primary	The science curriculum in KS4 may be organized in different ways, e.g. separate sciences rather than integrated/combined	Most of the reasons for the KS2 → KS3 dip apply here if pupils are transferring to a college	The change to AS has now made transition less of an issue
The learning environment in secondary science, e.g. laboratories, is different			
Pupils come from a range of feeder schools so range of teaching and learning styles experienced is large	There are changes in grouping, e.g. setting/ability groupings	There is no obligation for feeder schools to transfer assessment and diagnostic information to colleges	Those continuing to A2 know the score, so transition is not as much of a problem as it is elsewhere
Pupils come with specific perceptions and expectations of practical work	Teacher expectations, e.g. of standards of work, accuracy, quantity and detail, may be different	Change in study skills and demands and expectations of A level study	More mature – can cope with changes and pressures
Pupils in secondary schools are taught by many new teachers instead of just one			

(Continued)

Table 2.2 (Continued)

From KS2 → KS3	From KS3 → KS4	From KS4 → sixth form study	From AS → A2
Pupils have to establish different and new friendship/peer groups	The KS3 strategy has varied and exciting approaches to T&L while T&L at KS4 remains boring	The language level required and the precision in practical work represent extra demands	
Levels of attainment received in Y7 may not be a reliable guide to ability in science			
Experiences of science in primary schools vary widely despite the National Curriculum	For some pupils, KS3 SATs represent just one more point of failure	Students are required to show self-organization and be accountable	
Y6 pupils were big fish in a little pond; now they are just one fish in a big sea	KS4 represents more choice (and a wider range of delivery modes)	For many, school is not now the principle organizing structure of their lives – they have jobs, girlfriends/boyfriends, etc.	
Y7 pupils repeat activities, skills and learning from Y6 without sufficient progression and challenge and get bored			

made in the past 10 years (Galton et al., 1999; Schagen and Kerr, 1999). The 'shock of the new' for pupils after transfer, in terms of changes in pedagogy and curriculum, may however have a much more significant and longer-term impact on pupils' learning in science than in other subjects and on attitudes to science.

Post-transfer regression: what research has to say

At York we carried out extensive reviews of research studies on transitions and transfers in science across the world, particularly those relevant to the UK. A succinct review has been provided as part of the ASE's research focus series (see Braund, 2006) and more extensive reviews can be found in journal articles (Braund, 2007; Braund and Hames, 2005; Braund et al. 2003). The research literature suggests four principal factors that help explain the decline in science learning performance and pupils' attitudes to science following transfer to secondary schools:

1 Pupils may repeat work done at primary school, often without sufficient increase in challenge, sometimes in the same context and using identical procedures (Galton et al., 1999; House of Commons Education Committee, 1995; Jarman, 1990; Morrison, 2000; SSCR, 1987).
2 Teaching environments, teaching styles and teachers' language are often very different in secondary schools compared with primary schools. They represent a change in learning culture to which pupils have difficulty adjusting (Hargreaves and Galton, 2002; Pointon, 2000).
3 Teachers in secondary schools often fail to make use of, or refer to, pupils' previous science learning experiences. Information supplied by primary schools on their pupils' previous attainments is rarely used effectively to plan curriculum experiences in the secondary school (Doyle and Hetherington, 1998; Nicholls and Gardner, 1999; Schagen and Kerr, 1999).
4 Teachers in secondary schools distrust the assessed levels of performance gained by pupils in national tests in science, taken by all pupils in England and Wales, at the end of primary school. As discussed earlier, teachers in secondary schools often claim these levels have been artificially inflated by intensive revision for these tests (Bunyan, 1998; Schagen and Kerr, 1999). This may be used by secondary teachers as justification for 'starting from scratch' when planning new learning (Nott and Wellington, 1999).

We found these factors are not unique to England. Studies elsewhere have identified similar problems, for example, in the USA (Anderson et al., 2000), Australia (Scharf and Schibeci, 1990) and Finland (Pietarinen, 2000).

Perhaps of all these factors the first, concerning repetition, is most crucial. In the late 1980s Ruth Jarman surveyed over 2000 pupils either side of the primary–secondary transfer in Northern Ireland to compare their experiences in science learning and their attitudes to school science. Her survey represented 10 per cent of the entire school population of the province at the time and remains one of the most significant and thorough studies of science at transfer ever conducted. Jarman found that many pupils claimed much of their primary work, even exactly the same experiments, was repeated in secondary schools. If repetition is reinforcement that develops both conceptual and procedural learning, as part of what we understand as the 'spiral curriculum' described in the pervious chapter, then this seems justifiable. But the problem is that some repetition simply ignores or denigrates what has gone before. In an extensive survey carried out for the Nuffield Foundation for Educational Research (NFER), Schagen and Kerr found that several heads of science in secondary schools said that, despite science having been taught as a National Curriculum subject for several years, they would assume that pupils entering Y7 would have little or highly variable knowledge and experience of science and so they would adopt a 'clean slate' approach (Schagen and Kerr, 1999: 37–8). One question that seems to emerge from these findings is how do pupils react to repetition? Do they learn to tolerate it or does it quickly erode the generally positive attitudes that they have to science at the start of secondary school? The demotivating effect that repetition can have is shown starkly by this comment sent by email from a Y7 pupil to the Y6 pupils in her old primary school: 'I used to like science but here we started from scratch' (Morrison, 2000: 47).

In a study of 144 16-year-olds' recollections of, and attitudes to, school science by Osborne and Collins, one of the most negative comments about experiences of school science centred on repetition (Osborne and Collins, 2001). Pupils viewed repetition negatively in two ways:

1 From the point of view of repeated tests to prove the same point, for example, colour changes of indicators with acids/alkalis. According to Osborne and Collins this is repetition to persuade pupils of the validity of a world view but without addressing why it matters.
2 Repetition of topics without increasing depth from primary to secondary school and from lower to upper school. Excitement of new things in Y7 (atoms, molecules and electrons) but boredom and demotivation through repetition in every subsequent year.

From the above it seems that repetition remains a key issue not just at transfers but in year to year and topic to topic transitions, and that it has a long-lasting impact on attitudes. I discuss the implications of this more fully in the next chapter.

Finally it is worth considering what research has to say about the issue of language in science across the KS2/3 transfer. In 1999 Graham Peacock, working out of Sheffield Hallam University, presented results from a study commissioned by the Qualifications and Curriculum Authority (QCA) (Peacock, 1999). In his study, Peacock asked teachers from three clusters of primary and secondary schools in three different local education authorities (LEAs) what concepts, terms and words associated with plants and changes of state they would expect their pupils to know and understand. As expected he found an increase in numbers and complexity of terms used from KS1 to

KS2 but there was a *marked decrease* from KS2 to KS3. There were a striking number of cases where more teachers in primary schools expected an understanding of terms such as melting and boiling point, evaporate, and molecule than did their secondary counterparts receiving pupils a few months later. Regression in language is not unique to science, similar regression was evident in English lessons in the ORACLE study (Galton et al., 1999). Words in science, however, are important vehicles for conceptual understanding, and the findings are yet another example of how much the progress made in primary science is often under-appreciated by secondary schools. Peacock's study highlights a problem that the project teams at York took on board in the design of bridging materials. In later chapters I will show how the issue of continuity and progression in use of science language has been addressed, and evidence from pupils and teachers showing that this has been successful.

〰 Reflection

Write commonly used science words such as evaporation, condensation, solution, solute, digestion, variation, acceleration, gravity and density onto separate cards. Ask teachers of different year groups or key stages to say what understanding of these terms/concepts they would expect from the pupils they teach.

Doing something about post-transfer regression

In 1998 the Centre for Study of Comprehensive Schools (CSCS) issued questionnaires to delegates at their regional conferences to establish what was commonly done to address post-transfer regression and, more generally, to help pupils settle into their new schools. The results were analysed by Galton's research team and presented in an influential report on KS2/3 transfer to the Department for Education and Skills (Galton et al., 1999: 22–8). Galton summarized efforts to improve transfer as what have been called a series of 'bridges'. The first column of Table 2.3 shows frequencies of schools' actions in each of four bridges in 1999. Galton commented on the large effort being made in administrative, social and bureaucratic areas but the relatively low incidence of work to address continuity and progression of curriculum and/or pedagogy. Since schools were asked only to report initiatives introduced in the last few years and response rates were about 60 per cent of schools, the figures probably overestimated the real level of actions on curriculum and pedagogy.

Galton's report celebrated the successes of efforts made at that stage but, in view of much of the research reported in this chapter, he also called for much more effort to be made to tackle discontinuities and disruptions in teaching and learning. Specifically, Galton's report recommended:

- That there should be an array of tried and evaluated strategies, matched to specific experiences of transfer and transition, that schools could adapt for use in their own settings.
- Interested schools should be involved in developing post-transfer strategies that achieve good balance between academic and social concerns and that underline the importance of helping pupils to take learning seriously in school and become professional in their approaches to learning.
- Schools could be engaged in the development of teaching and learning strategies in particular subject areas that help pupils sustain their excitement in learning through experiences of transfer and transition and encourage those who, for whatever reason, are disengaged or disengaging, to get back on board.
- Schools should be supported in giving attention to pupils' accounts of why they disengage or under-perform at critical moments, for example following key transfers and transitions.
- Schools should collaborate to research for themselves what factors seem to influence pupils' progress and attitudes to learning and to translate findings into strategies that other schools can use. (Galton et al., 1999: 32)

〰 **Reflection**

> List all the actions that take place to smooth transfers and transitions in your institution. How do these compare with the actions identified by Galton et al.?

The survey used by CSCS was repeated in 2002 and findings are shown in Table 2.3. Comparisons with the 1999 data show there had been a marked increase in the use of initiatives to address curriculum issues but a much smaller increase in the use of strategies which, in Galton's view, address pedagogy more directly. Galton reports that the most significant driver for change in practice between 1999 and 2002 was the number of schools using 'bridging units'. These are usually planned episodes of work started in the last few weeks of primary school and progressed and completed shortly after pupils have transferred to secondary school. This approach has been developed for science by the York teams and is the subject of Chapter 6. Other strategies to address pedagogic, administrative and social aspects of transfer are discussed in detail by Celia Moore in Chapter 5. Later chapters show how some of the pedagogic strategies mentioned in Table 2.3, such as co-teaching, and co-observation of teaching, have been developed and what other strategies can be used in this area.

Table 2.3 Actions by schools to smooth KS2 → KS3 transfer

Area of initiatives	Examples	% of schools in 1999	% of schools in 2002
Administrative	Meetings, transfer of data, communication with parents	90	6
Social	Induction and open days, buddying and mentoring	50	32
Curriculum	Joint training, bridging work, summer schools	<20	46
Pedagogic	Teacher exchanges, shared or focused observation of teaching, joint teaching	2	9

Sources: Galton et al., 1999; 2003b

 Summary

In spite of a spirally constructed curriculum that should ensure continuity and progression across key stages, it is evident that in science there is significant regression for many pupils following transfer to secondary school. Research shows that principal causes lie in the lack of awareness of progress previously made and particularly practical procedures, concepts and language already met and understood. As a result, teaching is repetitive, which pupils resent. Strategies to address post-transfer regression have tended to concentrate on helping pupils to settle into new classes after transfer and these appear to have been successful. There recently has been a marked increase in the use of bridging work but there has been less effort to address pedagogy directly, for example, through the use of co-teaching or co-observation of teaching.

Suggested actions

- Use the list of practical activities commonly used in primary schools, provided in the Text Box 2.1.
- Place participants (teachers, students or other educators) in pairs. One with experience of primary school, and the other with experience of secondary school, science. Ask participants to tick any activity that they might commonly use in teaching.
- Ask participants to compare their selections.
- Pick one activity that both participants say they use and first ask the person with primary experience to say what they would expect pupils to do and to achieve from carrying out the activity.
- Repeat the above for the person with experience of secondary teaching.

Text Box 2.1

Please Miss/Sir, we've done this before!

Which of these do you include in your teaching?	Tick ✓
Investigating pulse rates	
Measuring human variations, e.g. height, arm/leg length, eye colour	
Dissecting flowers	
Investigating the germination of seeds	
Using keys to identify invertebrates ('minibeasts')	
Exploring seed dispersal	
Exploring decay (the growth of moulds)	
Paper chromatography	
Filtering dirty water	
Testing the strength of materials (e.g. paper)	
Stretching materials with different loads (e.g. rubber bands, springs)	
Factors affecting dissolving	
Mixing vinegar and bicarbonate of soda	
Testing friction (e.g. friction of trainers)	
Investigating parachutes	
Making parallel circuits	
How to make a bulb in a circuit brighter	
Changing the size of a shadow	
Changing the pitch of a sound	
Observing reflection patterns	

Source: adapted from activities first published in DfES, 2002b.

3

Moving to the Big School:
Part 1 – Children's Voices

Chapter overview

The design of questionnaires to collect evidence from pupils' voices is discussed and two examples are provided. The pupil voice either side of transfer is reviewed from four perspectives to shed light on how KS2/3 transfer might be smoothed and improved. A discussion on the implications of pupils' voices for the development of school science, particularly for a more authentic curriculum to develop scientific literacy, closes the chapter.

It is easy to make assumptions about what is best for pupils. Research on pupil performance and studies of curriculum content and progression help us design schemes of work we think are the best we can offer but there is no effective short cut to finding out what is really being experienced – we have to ask the subjects and supposed beneficiaries of all this effort – the pupils themselves. In recent years there has been an increasing emphasis in education on listening to and taking account of the pupil/student voice. Perhaps this is a result of the 'consumer-rights' approach that seems to have crept into education through the market-driven approach to education, and some readers might feel uncomfortable with this. On the other hand, there is now a broadening consensus that taking account of the pupil voice is an essential and natural part of school improvement. In a book dealing mainly with transitions and transfers, Rudduck et al. noted that: 'Schools do not adequately take account of the tensions and pressures that pupils feel as they struggle to reconcile the demands of their social and personal lives with their development and identity as learners' (1996: 1).

More recently school inspections in England have adopted a slimmed-down system requiring shorter inspection visits that rely heavily on schools' self-evaluation of their own progress as the basis for inspection. As part of this, schools are required to provide evidence of pupils' views of teaching and learning (Ofsted, 2005). The precise methods for gathering data for self evaluation are left up to schools but guidance makes clear that pupils' views are of paramount importance:

> It is up to each school to decide precisely who should be consulted and how views are gathered. The involvement of learners, parents and support agencies in the self evaluation process is essential. Evidence can be collected in a range of ways, for example through surveys, focus groups, the school council, annual reviews and interviews. In some schools, students are invited to observe and evaluate lessons. (Ofsted, 2004a: para 23, 9)

First, I review the principles of collecting quality information on pupils' attitudes to science, providing a questionnaire that has been well researched and discussed in the hope that this might guide and help self-evaluation. In the rest of the chapter I review pupils' voices either side of the primary–secondary transfer from four key perspectives:

1 Pupils' general attitudes to science.
2 Pupils' aspirations and concerns about learning and doing science at secondary school.
3 Perceptions of the differences between primary and secondary experiences.
4 Pupils' perceptions of and attitudes to the nature and purposes of practical work in science.

Pupils' attitudes to practical work in science lessons are treated separately as this is an area that looms large in the experiences of pupils either side of transfer, and so pupils' voices have importance in planning for effective actions to reduce regression and smooth transitions.

Collecting evidence of pupils' attitudes to science

In reviewing research on pupils' attitudes to science, Bennett (2003: 181–2) reminds us of the confusion and lack of clarity about what constitutes pupils' attitudes. She suggests five different strands against which data might usefully be collected. These include pupils' dispositions towards:

- school science
- science in the world outside school
- the relevance and importance of science to everyday life
- scientists and the ways in which they work
- scientific careers.

In work carried out for the AstraZeneca Science Teaching Trust (AZSTT), Pell and Jarvis devised a set of statements to measure attitude on these dispositions. Their methodology is described fully in a paper in the *International Journal of Science Education* (Pell and Jarvis, 2001) and a simplified version of their survey questionnaire is available for download on the AZSTT website (www.azteachscience.co.uk/code/az/project/cognitive/attitudes.html).

Research teams at York selected a few items from the full survey but that still do the job of collecting information against the dispositions listed by Bennett. This version is provided as Text Box 3.1. We tested this shortened version with a wider range of ages than Pell and Jarvis used, and found that a particular set of items (1, 3, 5, 7, 8, 9, 10, 12 and 14) hang together as a coherent set to measure attitude to science (Braund et al., 2007). Remaining questions still provide interesting individual sets of data for schools' self-evaluations. We found that the three 'smiley faces' system seems to work particularly well for pupils in primary and lower secondary classes. The statement at the top of the sheet can be used by the teacher as an example to show pupils how to fill in the sheet. Rather oddly, we found that most pupils seemed to agree with this statement (scientists all want to destroy the world) even when they responded positively to most other items!

Findings from using this questionnaire with about 500 pupils confer with many of those discussed in the rest of this chapter though one interesting difference is that in our work we have found a very sharp increase, compared with previous studies (for example, Craig and Ayers, 1988), in interest in reading about science. This is something worth pursuing in the design of lessons and schemes of work either side of transfer.

 Reflection

Should pupils evaluate teaching? How can information on the 'pupil voice' be collected effectively and sensitively in schools in order to improve learning?

Pupils' general attitudes to science

According to Bennett (2003: 174–94) the patterns evident from many studies on pupil attitudes to science, and in particular school science, in the UK and elsewhere, are remarkably similar. The picture is one of relatively positive attitudes at and following transfer, followed by progressive decline as pupils move through secondary school. Part of the problem seems to be that pupils begin to see science as irrelevant to and divorced from everyday life. Oddly, perhaps it seems that the downturn in attitude in secondary schools is not necessarily connected with the amount of science done at primary level. In an early study on this, Craig and Ayers found that pupils from primary

Text Box 3.1

What I think about science

In this part you have to tick or colour **just one smiley face** for each line – like this:

	Agree	Not sure	Disagree
Scientists all want to destroy the world	☺	☺	☹ ✔

Here are some views about science. Tick one smiley face for each statement:

		Agree	Not sure	Disagree
1	Science is good for everyone	☺	☺	☹
2	Lots more money should be spent on science	☺	☺	☹
3	I like science more than most other lessons	☺	☺	☹
4	Science has made better and safer medicines	☺	☺	☹
5	I am quite good at science	☺	☺	☹
6	TV, DVDs and mobile phones all needed science to help make them	☺	☺	☹
7	We have to do too much work in science	☺	☺	☹
8	I would like to be a scientist	☺	☺	☹
9	I like to watch science programmes on TV	☺	☺	☹
10	Science is too hard	☺	☺	☹
11	Science can make chemicals from rocks	☺	☺	☹
12	I like reading about science	☺	☺	☹
13	Scientists work in laboratories most of the time	☺	☺	☹
14	Scientists are rather 'geeky' or 'sad people'	☺	☺	☹

schools doing relatively 'high' amounts of science were no more likely to produce pupils liking science and wanting to continue with it after transfer than schools teaching 'low' amounts of science (Craig and Ayers, 1988). In fact the girls in their study were more likely to have been put off by having done more science in primary school. In more recent research quoted by Galton et al. (2003b), there seems to be evidence of a widening gap in the decline of attitudes among girls, a feature noted in earlier studies of science transition in Australia (Speering and Rennie, 1996). Speculatively we might assume that this could be an effect of repetition of work discussed in the previous chapter, although another study suggested that in some cases girls might actually be more tolerant of repeated work than are boys (Braund and Driver, 2005a). Clearly this is an area for schools to continue to explore in their own self-evaluations.

Pupils' views on the difficulty and challenge of science work are worth considering. In research by Galton (2002) it seems that, for some pupils, the excitement of and enthusiasm for science shortly after transfer has worn off by the end of Y7. Work in Suffolk LA shows that disaffection may be greatest for most able pupils, who perceive much Y7 science work as being under-challenging (Suffolk County Council Education Department, 2002b). Similar fears about the lack of challenges facing pupils transferring to junior high schools have been voiced in studies from the USA and Australia, where this has been linked to increased delinquent behaviour (Eccles and Midgeley, 1989; Speering and Rennie, 1996).

Naturally, teachers might assume that their highest performing pupils are also those with the most positive dispositions for and liking of science. According to Galton et al. this relationship cannot be reliably assumed. They found that in science tests in Y7 and again through Y8 and Y9, the pupils who performed best often had the poorest attitudes to science (Galton et al., 2003b). Motivation levels of these pupils were high – they wanted to do well – but only to prove that they could pass the tests and do well in future examinations – not because they liked science as a subject. Galton et al. refer to this as 'storing up trouble for the future' (2003b: 57). International comparisons such as TIMSS (Trends in International Mathematics and Science Study) confirm that in countries where high average achievement in science is seen (Japan, Korea, Taipei, Hong Kong) pupils' attitudes to science are least positive (Martin et al., 2000).

Pupils' aspirations and concerns about learning and doing science at secondary school

In studies at York, we used focus group interviews to uncover pupils' general attitudes to science and, more specifically, their aspirations and fears on doing science at secondary school. Interviews were carried out in the last few weeks of Y6 and some of the pupils were interviewed again after about eight to 10 weeks in their secondary schools. Results for general liking of science in Y6 showed the same levels of positive response discussed above and were stable across groups from two different LAs. There were no differences between boys and girls or between types of school – small or large, urban or rural. Only seven out of 59 pupils interviewed made any negative comments, and these pupils spoke positively about at least one aspect of science such as practical work. This positive attitude to practical science dominates and was a common feature in over half of all positive comments:

> I like the activities ... you know where you get to do all that stuff testing things and especially when we tested differences ... (Boy, Y6)

> The experiments, when you are physically doing something, that's OK. Girl (Y6)

Negative comments were often associated with having to produce writing, sometimes in contrast to doing practical work:

> Well, it's sometimes boring when you have to do writing and stuff like that. (Girl 1, Y6)

> Yes, I like it when you do experiments but I don't like it when you have to write loads after. (Girl 2, Y6)

Out of the 32 pupils who were re-interviewed following transfer, attitudes (liking for science) remained positive. There was little evidence of the sorts of dips in attitude mentioned above and this might be because these pupils had followed a programme of bridging work, although the studies discussed earlier used different research instruments and were carried out in different geographic locations so direct comparisons are not really valid.

When it came to looking forward to science in secondary school, comments on practical work were again dominant. Responses most commonly referred to working in a laboratory, doing more and different practicals and using new equipment (Bunsen burners featured the most – see the next section). Some pupils also mentioned the excitement of doing new topics – mainly in chemistry, and this was again linked to opportunities to use new equipment or to handle chemicals.

Pupils' concerns and anxieties about doing secondary science are summarized in Table 3.1. Each expression of anxiety about transfer in science, including statements showing that these were of no real concern or could be addressed by some action, was coded using a computer programme (Nvivo – see Glossary). We followed the same pupils after transfer to see what had happened to their worries. As far as we know, this part of the study is unique in research into KS2/3 transfer.

The overall pattern was that most anxieties expressed by Y6 pupils dissipate soon after transfer, although some safety concerns remained. It appears that this might be because a new procedure or piece of equipment presents new risks and fears that could not have been anticipated. Here is what Alex (a boy) said about this before and after transfer:

> I would be worried if I was doing the experiments where you are mixing chemicals together and they would explode in your face. (Alex, in Y6)

> When I'm using a Bunsen burner, if someone knocks it over while we are using it and it sets something on fire. (Alex, in Y7)

Table 3.1 Frequency of comments made by pupils about studying science before and after transfer

Coded response 'node'	Frequency of response	
	Y6	Y7
Writing worries	1	0
Worried about getting it wrong	6	1
Language worries	0	1
Worried about safety	12	11
No worries – more exciting	1	2
No worries – positive expectations	2	0
No worries – now	0	6
No worries – induction	8	0
No worries – not as hard as expected	0	2

Note: 32 pupils were interviewed but each pupil may have expressed several views

It could also be that the experience of introductory topics, where pupils learn the rules and protocols of laboratory work, are particularly dominant in the first term of secondary schools and so have a marked impact on what pupils see as important. Michael Reiss's famous, five-year longitudinal study of science lessons supports this view, and I think his account of the first few weeks in secondary school seen through the eyes of the pupil, teacher and researcher is well worth reading (Reiss, 2000).

There were a number of concerns which we coded as 'worried about getting it wrong' even though some of these were still about experimental procedures. For example:

I'm worried that the teachers are going to yell at you if you don't do it in time. (Amy, Y6)

If it gets too complicated and you don't understand anything and you are like, mixing chemicals and you like say 'are we supposed to use this one because I've lost my instruction card'? (Lewis, Y6)

It was pleasing to note that these concerns seemed to have disappeared soon after transfer. This might reflect an increasing confidence among pupils and a patient, sympathetic and tolerant attitude by Y7 teachers to the mistakes made by new entrants. Finally, there was a significant minority of responses from pupils that seemed to confirm that induction programmes or visits to secondary school allay fears about moving on:

We did a visit on Friday and everyone was in different science groups and I was with Mrs N and when we went in, everyone was in pairs, and she told us to build a rocket and put one spoonful into a camera case, where your film goes in, and put 5 cm of water in and put the lid on quickly before the gas came out and soon, in about 5 seconds, it will pop up. Then we had to design our own rocket. (Hollie, Y6)

The levels of detail remembered about this particular visit suggest that liaison visits and induction days such as this one are valuable. They are discussed in detail in Chapter 5.

Differences between primary and secondary experiences of science

As part of her extensive studies in Northern Ireland, Ruth Jarman surveyed 1767 pupils at the end of their first term in secondary schools asking what they perceived now as the main differences between science in their second-ary and primary schools (Jarman, 1993). The key findings of her study were:

- More pupils quoted differences in work than they did similarities.
- Many pupils gave examples of topics that were the same as those studied before; the natural world being most frequent, for example, animals (12.2 per cent), water (8.6 per cent).
- 27 per cent of pupils said that they had done the same/similar activities as in primary school. Many said they repeated exactly the same experiments.
- Only a quarter recognized similarity in procedures and processes of science.
- One of the most frequent and unsolicited categories of comments was about learning safety rules. Significantly more boys gave this response.
- Working with different equipment and in laboratory settings were the most commonly mentioned differences. 62 per cent mentioned the Bunsen burner.
- Pupils commonly regarded secondary science as: sophisticated, real/proper (14 per cent) science rather than play.
- Some secondary pupils claimed that they now took more responsibility in practical work.
- 20 per cent remarked on an increase in depth of study in secondary science. Girls were more likely to say this.

Some findings are consistent with those already discussed. The dominance of practical work in the minds of pupils at transfer is again evident. Jarman even goes as far as to call using the Bunsen burner 'a rite of passage into the realm of "real" (*sic.* secondary science)' (1993: 23). What pupils see as purposes of science practical work and the issues that arise from such work for curricu-lum design and actions to smooth transitions are discussed in the next sec-tion. The issue of repetition of work and the demotivation that this can bring about has been commented on in the previous chapter and is, of course, a dominant theme of this book. Another issue of continuity and progression arises from the findings that pupils perceive science in secondary school as more different than it is similar to what has been experienced before. If science is a learning continuum, drawing on similar sets of skills and processes of science, or procedural knowledge as we called this in Chapter 1, then it could be argued that there ought to be some recognition of continuity of experience. The thesis of the National (spiral) Curriculum is that similar sets of procedures are developed in new and more demanding (abstract and more conceptually advanced) contexts. Perhaps the experiences of many pupils is that science in secondary schools is now so different because it is being regarded as 'proper and real' and so their view is that procedures, though practised (played at?) before, are now somehow more authenticated as part of doing 'real' or 'proper' science. Some schools have operated schemes of induction into science in Y7 with titles such as 'being a scientist' or 'starting science'. The treatment of science as new or 'from scratch' is reinforced when secondary teachers adopt views like 'real science starts with us' or 'you can forget all that stuff you did in the primary school – that was just playing at science'. Fortunately such overt references that denigrate the worth of primary science are rare. I discuss the positive impact that bridging work can have in promoting science as a 'learning continuum' in Chapters 6 and 7.

The classroom environment and differences in pedagogy can both impact on post-transfer learning. In a study by Pointon (2000), pupils were interviewed about how they saw their learning environment changing since primary school. Greater independence of working (in pairs rather than in larger groups) and the chance to identify with new subject titles were viewed favourably. The lack of pupils' work displayed or the fact that classroom displays and posters seemed irrelevant to their year group or topics studied in Y7 were seen as negative aspects. Galton reported fewer open-ended questions used in Y7 science and a decline in use of group-focused tasks. Results from the ORACLE replication study described in Chapter 2 showed an increase in secondary classrooms in whole-class interactions but a decline in pupil–teacher interactions (Hargreaves and Galton, 2002). All of the above add up to a negative impact on pupils' learning but, perhaps most seriously, an extensive study for NFER revealed that pupils reported far fewer opportunities for them to talk about their work with teachers in secondary compared with primary schools (Keys et al., 1995). Hopefully this situation is now being addressed by moves to introduce more formative and diagnostic assessment methods into secondary school work (see, for example, suggestions made by Black et al., 2002).

〰 Reflection

How do explanations for pupils' declining attitudes in science given so far in this chapter fit with your own experiences? What other explanations can be offered?

Pupils' perceptions of and attitudes to the nature and purposes of practical work in science

The importance of practical work in pupils' views of school science is a dominant theme of research quoted so far. As a prelude to designing bridging units in science (see Chapter 6) the project and research teams at York decided that more information was needed about pupils' specific views on the nature and purposes of practical work either side of transfer. We decided that scientific enquiries contained in the bridging materials described in Chapter 6 would be best framed in commercial or industrial contexts. Our warrant for this comes from previous experience with a number of projects and from research that leads to a view that science is often successful for, and more attractive, to pupils when they can see 'relevance' for their studies. A review of research on context-based and science–technology–society (STS) approaches confirms that they are indeed motivating and have a positive effect on pupils' attitudes to science (Bennett et al., 2003). If contexts for practical science used either side of transfer are to be successful in terms of impact, motivation and ultimately pupil learning, attitudes to practical science both in school and in the workplace are worth exploring. While we know something about the, often stereotypical and restricted, view that pupils have of scientists and their roles and that these views are well established even at primary age (Newton and Newton, 1998), we know much less about what pupils think about why people use practical science in their work and how this compares with pupils' views of school science.

A simple questionnaire was devised to elicit pupils' responses on these matters. This is shown as Text Box 3.2. The questionnaire was given to 13 teachers, eight teaching primary classes and five teaching in secondary schools. The schools were considered to be broadly representative of all types and sizes of schools in the LA where the study took place. Consistent with other research, November was chosen as a good time to carry out the study in both sets of schools as pupils would have had a chance to settle into new ways of working.

Pupils' views on practical science in schools

Summaries of responses to two of the questions: 'why do pupils do practical science at school?', and 'what might be/is different about practical science in primary and secondary school?', are provided in Table 3.2 and Table 3.3 respectively.

Unsurprisingly, large proportions of both primary and secondary pupils thought that practical work would contribute positively to their general learning in science. A noticeable proportion of those who claimed this (about a fifth) also believed that practical work provided a useful independent experience that supports learning. The following response was typical:

> I think that pupils do practical science at school because they can find things out for themselves rather than the teacher telling them. It's more fun than just the teacher showing them. (Y6 pupil)

Text Box 3.2

Questionnaire used to collect pupils' views on science practical work

Why do pupils do practical science (tests, investigations, experiments) at school?

What might be/is the **same** about practical science in primary and secondary schools?

What might be/is **different** about practical science in primary and secondary schools?

Why do some people do practical science as part of their jobs?

What is the **same** about the practical science people do in their jobs and the practical science pupils do at school?

What is **different** about the practical science that people do in their jobs and the practical science pupils do at school?

Please tell me your age in years and months: ⎯⎯⎯⎯⎯⎯⎯⎯⎯

*Are you in a primary school □ *or secondary school? □

*Are you a boy □ or a girl? □

*Please tick a box

Thank you for helping us

☺

Similar proportions (around 20 per cent) of Y6 and Y7 pupils stated that practical work made studying science fun, enjoyable or motivating. Some responses were qualified by pupils, who added that at least practical work was preferable to learning science by other means, for example, through reading or written work, a feature picked up in later studies at York.

> (We do practical work in science) ... because it helps you better if you do science yourself rather than read it from a book. (Y6 pupil)

The most noticeable difference in responses from the two groups of pupils concerned their perceptions of what future benefits practical science might bring. Surprisingly, Y6 pupils were much more likely than their Y7 counterparts to see practical science as useful in improving job prospects. Twenty-nine pupils in Y6 claimed this, yet only one pupil in Y7 classes did so. Year 6 pupils were also surer that practical science might help further study:

> If you want to be a scientist or work as a doctor you have to be good at science. (Y6 pupil)

Table 3.2 Analysis of Y6 and Y7 pupils' responses to Q1: why do pupils do practical science (tests, investigations, experiments) at school?

Response category	Y6 pupils			Y7 pupils		
	Total (%) (n = 117)	Girls (%) (n = 76)	Boys (%) (n = 41)	Total (%) (n = 105)	Girls (%) (n = 52)	Boys (%) (n = 53)
To find out or learn more	63	58	73	75	90	60
For a job/to be a scientist	25	24	27	1	0	2
Fun, enjoyable, interesting, motivating and/ or better than learning by other means	21	23	20	18	24	14
Helps in our future learning and/or study	15	12	20	5	10	0
To use or apply skills or learn to carry out practical science	9	5	15	1	2	0

Source: Braund and Driver, 2005a: 83

> I think pupils at school do practical science so they can begin to decide if they like science and if they want to do a job that has science as part of their job. (Y6 pupil)

> When we do investigations it's to learn and if you get a job and you do chemistry or you might get a test on it in secondary school. (Y6 pupil)

Such positive, career-oriented opinions of school science have been found among older pupils, for example, at age 16, but rarely at this age (Osborne and Collins, 2001). Although numbers were small, just six pupils in the Y7 sample, a few pupils were already aware that practical work might be important in future examination success.

> (We do practical work in science) because it helps us learn and it works us up to our GCSEs. (Y7 pupil)

> When we do investigations ... if you do chemistry ... you might get a test on it in secondary school. (Y6 pupil)

Such opinions might reflect covert messages given by teachers especially if that teacher's view of practical work is dominated by assessment. Research

Table 3.3 Analysis of Y6 and Y7 pupils' responses to Q3: what might be/is *different* about practical science in primary and secondary schools?

Response category	Y6 pupils			Y7 pupils		
	Total (%) (n = 117)	Girls (%) (n = 76)	Boys (%) (n = 41)	Total (%) (n = 105)	Girls (%) (n = 52)	Boys (%) (n = 53)
Use different/ better/more equipment	35	35	32	23	25	21
Work is/will be harder or more advanced	40	41	39	11	17	6
Do more (some) experiments	5	5	5	29	33	25
Do more dangerous work (use more dangerous chemicals)	29	25	34	22	37	8
Work in a laboratory or specialist area	14	14	12	1	1	0

Source: Braund and Driver, 2005a: 83

into teacher's opinions on the National Curriculum for science and how it has influenced their use of practical work (Donnelley, 2000; Jenkins, 2000), suggests that some science teachers regard curriculum requirements for practical work as a straitjacket, focused mainly on practical work (fair-test type investigations) whose main purpose is to help pupils gain good grades in examinations. Though numbers of pupils who explicitly referred to practical work in this way were few in this study the message, 'being good at practical work will stand you in good stead for future success', may already be part of the classroom culture in Y7 classes. Thus the motivation to do well, as Galton found, is *extrinsic*, that is, to succeed in examinations, rather than *intrinsic*, brought by a personal sense of enjoyment of the work.

A comment, made by a significantly greater number of pupils in Y7 (30/105) than in Y6 (6/117) was that at least they were now doing more practical work in science than they had in primary school. Pupils' changing expectations and experience may have coloured their views as to what they now perceive as 'practical work', and it may be that pupils are now less inclined, after three months in a Y7 class, to accept teacher demonstrations and short-term tasks as 'proper' practical work. There were a few instances where pupils explicitly compared the nature of the practical work that they experienced in Y7 with that at Y6. The following comment made by one Y7 pupil is worth noting.

> Nothing is the same (about practical science in Y7 and Y6) because in primary school all you do is mini-experiments and in secondary school you do really good experiments which are big. (Y7 pupil)

On the other hand there was evidence that not much practical work was done at all in Y6.

> At primary school we didn't do experiments just sheets and we had no equipment. (Y7 pupil)

> In secondary school we do practicals and in primary schools we don't (Y7 pupil)

Other work at York (Braund and Hames, 2005) and surveys carried out for the National Union of Teachers (Galton and MacBeath, 2002) and by the Association for Science Education (ASE, 1999) all suggest a decline in the amount of time being spent on science teaching and in particular on practical work in Y6. This is attributed largely to the introduction into primary schools in England and Wales of national teaching strategies in literacy and numeracy and on pressures of high stakes national testing at the end of the primary school and consequent publication and comparison of schools' results forcing teachers to spend more time on revision (Galton and Macbeath, 2002).

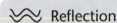 Reflection

What are the purposes of practical work in science? Should practical work feature equally in Y6 and Y7?

Pupils' views on practical work in the world of work

Similar and quite large proportions (> 30 per cent) of pupils in both year groups claimed that people engaged in practical science did so because they enjoyed using it or liked finding things out. Some pupils in both phases gave types of discoveries aided by practical investigation. The most frequent examples were of a medical nature, for example, to discover new medicines or cures. The following response was typical:

> (People do practical science as part of their jobs) ... 'So new medicines can be made and cures can be found and studied so that there are more chances of people living longer'. (Y7 pupil)

A striking difference between Y6 and Y7 concerned the extent to which pupils were likely to state that people use practical work in their jobs in testing products or procedures. Though numbers were small, primary pupils were much more likely to state this.

> Scientists do it (use practical science in their jobs) to prove what they have discovered. Cosmetic people test make-up to make sure people will

not be allergic to it. Basically, they test things all the time to find out something. (Y6 pupil)

It seems that primary pupils are more likely to make connections between science and product manufacture or testing and more generally to every- . day and commercial contexts than their secondary counterparts.

There was a general impression among pupils that 'doing science' is defined by practical work and so anyone engaged in its pursuit must naturally carry it out. The interesting feature here is that it was the primary pupils in Y6 who were much more likely to state this. The findings here, taken along with those discussed above, seem to suggest that, Y6 pupils in particular operate in a frame that sees practical work as generally useful and enjoyable and a natural consequence of scientific endeavour, whether this be for learning in school or as part of a job. This provides some justification for framing transition activities including bridging work in contexts that are familiar to pupils and that encourage them to see science as an authentic and every-day activity linked to finding solutions that affect people.

Implications for science education and for pupils' scientific literacy

According to research carried out for the Royal Society, many scientists establish their liking for science before the age of 14. In many cases motivation to do science could be traced back before age 12 (Royal Society, 2006a). A different report bemoans the continuing decline in the UK of recruits into further science studies in sixth forms, recruitment to university courses in the physical sciences and into careers involving engineering, physics and electronics (Royal Society 2006b). Similar patterns can be identified in other industrialized nations of the Northern Hemisphere and in Australia. Thus attitudes to science matter and are established early. What is experienced in the years around primary–secondary transfer is crucial.

To me what emerges most strongly from pupils' voices discussed in this chapter is that most enter secondary schools with positive views and attitudes towards school science and to science and society. In other words, we can assume that primary science experience has done a reasonably good job or that at least it has not eroded children's natural curiosity and/or the positive influences of out-of-school experience. It is clear that pupils have high expectations of secondary science. To most it is an exciting opportunity, and the apprehensions about doing it soon disappear after a few weeks of practice and settling in. Many teachers might think that children are just being lazy when they say they like science and practical work until they have to produce something on paper. Of course, practical work might be popular because it represents a sort of relative mental 'downtime' and a chance to socialize with peers, but I think there is more to it than this. According to studies of group discussions during and about practical activity, most pupils enjoy group work and the chance to talk because it provides a chance to rehearse developing ideas and change them in a safer and more flexible environment than having to write something down (Barnes and Todd, 1995). It appears, however, that the chances to do this and to have contributions made in writing celebrated as displays diminish in secondary classrooms. Perhaps there are some key messages here about what types of classroom environments might be usefully provided following transfer.

Partly because of the trends discussed in this chapter, science educators in many countries have expressed concerns that science lessons in schools at the secondary level are all too often boring, irrelevant and outdated, designed mainly to educate a minority of future scientists, rather than equipping the majority with the scientific understanding, reasoning and literacy they require to engage as citizens in the twenty-first century (Goodrum et al., 2001; Millar and Osborne, 1998; Sjøberg, 1997). In this move towards what some call 'scientific literacy' (Millar, 2006) or in providing 'democratic access to aid social and political interaction' (Braund and Reiss, 2006), the role of scientists in examining the validity and reliability of claims and theories, and the evidence on which they are based, becomes as important as gaining knowledge about scientific principles and concepts. Key to this view of science is placing what is studied in lessons in the types of contexts that pupils of this age (11–12) might find interesting and so engage with: debate about harmful radiation from mobile phones, why fizzy drinks taste sweeter when they go flat, how to design and test safe bungee-jumps, and so on. Some educators see science education as more *authentic* when quality time is spent exploring such problems in some depth (Roth, 1997). Sadly, it is beyond current reality to expect that primary schools, at least in England, can provide the type of educational environment in which these longer-term and authentic projects might flourish. In England the notion of lengthy and integrated topic work in primary schools was criticized because subject objectives for learning were said to be poorly identified and much of the work ended up being fragmented and demeaning (Alexander et al., 1992). Whatever the validity of these claims about topic work, and I have doubts about many of them, it is certainly true that high stakes national tests with the attendant need to publish results in league tables comparing schools has concentrated efforts in Y6 on revision regimes. Topic work and use of any practical work at all in science lessons, let alone anything long term, has all but disappeared in English primary schools. Perhaps this is why an increasing number of pupils at transfer see more discontinuity than continuity in the use and application of science process skills as they move into secondary classes.

The pressures to change science teaching fundamentally in Key Stage 3 are great and, though progress might seem slow, there have been significant gains and changes in pedagogy particularly as promoted by the Key Stage 3 Strategy (Ofsted, 2004b; Stoll et al., 2003). The National Curriculum now contains a new section at Key Stage 4 (14–16) called 'How science works' that offers opportunities to promote the development of the sorts of attributes that 'scientific literacy' and more 'authentic' school science requires

(DfEE/QCA, 1999: 37). Proposals for a new Key Stage 3 curriculum for science to be introduced in 2008 follow similar lines in extending 'How science works' and reducing content. It is to be hoped that taken together these changes in curriculum and different attitudes to pedagogy might encourage a move towards school science in the first few years of secondary schooling that is less content oriented, more relevant to the interests and needs of pupils, and has improved continuity in teaching following transfer. I return to some of these key policy issues in the final chapter.

Summary

Gathering pupils' views on their experiences of learning has become central to schools' self-evaluations and for school improvement. The pattern of pupils' attitudes to science is one of high expectation on entry to secondary schools followed by decline thereafter. On the positive side, anxieties about doing science after transfer quickly disappear. Pupils enjoy practical work in science and can often state why it is important at work, although the lack of awareness of continuity in procedures seems to indicate that practical work in science lacks clearly marked pathways of progression across the transfer. Pressures in Y6 seem to show the amount of time given to practical science is at best limited. In a move towards more authentic school science concerned with developing scientific literacy there is value in developing schemes that promote critical engagement with the types of knowledge required by the 'How science works' component of the National Curriculum.

Suggested actions

- Use questionnaires such as those shown in Text Boxes 3.1 and 3.2 to collect and compare data on pupils' attitudes to science, science in society and practical work.
- Secondary school science classrooms could be organized to provide more group discussions and regular displays of pupils' work.
- Include reading about science tasks and get pupils to contribute to a class or school science magazine. Include recent news items about science onto classroom displays.
- Think about setting topics for lessons in both Y6 and Y7 in contexts that are interesting and engaging for this age, and that clearly show the relevance of science to everyday life.
- Providing more experiences of practical work in Y6 will help pupils see practical skills and procedural knowledge in science as something they can always use and that naturally develops, rather than something that starts again in secondary schools.

4

Moving to the Big School: Part 2 – Teachers' Voices

> **Chapter overview**
>
> Responses to statements in a quiz designed to provoke debate on transfer issues are discussed. Insights on how teachers in primary and secondary schools see the use of supposedly common assessment criteria and contextualized teaching help guide development of bridging materials and other strategies to improve transfer in science.

I discussed general opinions on problems at key transitional points in science learning in Chapter 2. During and following the launch of bridging units (see Chapter 6) the team at York wanted to go deeper – to collect detailed information through the voices of teachers and others on the primary–secondary transfer. At dissemination events, conferences and workshops we used a true or false 'quiz' containing 10 statements and one open-response item designed to stimulate debate about approaches to teaching and learning and assessment of science in primary and secondary schools, and to elicit teachers' detailed knowledge and opinions concerning transfer.

The quiz was based on an activity used with secondary teachers attending training on transition in the national pilot of the science strand of the KS3 Strategy in the City of York and elsewhere during 2001–02 (see DfES, 2002b). A copy of our version of the 'quiz' is provided as Text Box 4.1. The exercise was also used during in-service training (Inset) sessions at local and national meetings of the Association for Science Education and in training events provided by the project team for LEA officers, consultants and teachers wishing to use the STAY project materials. The quiz was placed on the AstraZeneca Science Teaching Trust's website as part of a professional development unit (PDU) on KS2/3 transfer in science. This is a freely available resource and can be downloaded or used online. (see www.azteachscience .co.uk/code/development/stay.asp).

The quiz contains two types of statements; those having factual right/ wrong answers, for example, question (3) on when the National Curriculum for science was first introduced into all primary schools, and those designed to provoke debate where there is no right or wrong answer. The project team debated statements of this second type and came to a collective view. These views are shown by the ticks in the true/false boxes on the version of the quiz shown in Text Box 4.1. We also provided a summary of discussion for each statement to explain the reasoning behind our decisions. These 'answers' were provided for participants at the end of training events (see Text Box 4.2). In most cases the 'answers' heeded guidance produced for trainers involved in the Key Stage 3 Strategy (DfES, 2002b: 14–15). Statements (8), (9) and (10) were added to the original set in the Key Stage 3 pack to get responses that might inform the design of bridging units and because we wanted to raise these issues with participants who might go on to use them. The reader should note that it was not our intention to promote our team view/answer as a definitive or correct one. In training sessions we were careful to allow teachers to express their ideas and to justify them. We did the same. The result was that we often agreed to differ. For us, the process of engagement between primary and secondary teachers and the value of discussing each other's attitudes to the science curriculum and teaching were real and lasting benefits of the exercise.

Responses to the quiz statements were gathered from 71 primary teachers and 82 secondary teachers. The findings are shown in Table 4.1. Data corresponding to 'agreeing with' the team's view are shown in bold text.

Two key issues that emerged from analysis of responses shown in Table 4.1 and which are not discussed in great detail elsewhere in this book are explored here. Responses to the open question provided at the end of the quiz offer further insights on post-transfer regression.

Equitability of assessment

The first statement of the quiz was identical to one used in the Key Stage 3 Strategy training materials. The 'answer' suggested in the KS3 pack reads:

> True and false. There are conceptual aspects of level 4 that are exactly the same in Key Stage 3 as they are in Key Stage 2. However, the content of the Key Stage 3 programme is different to that in Key Stage 2. Detailed discussions about these subtle differences can be unhelpful and can distract from building on what pupils already know and can do. (DfES, 2002: 15)

While we agreed, in the main, with this statement we decided not to sit on the fence, and so we claimed that the statement was true. We reasoned that the assessment model in the National Curriculum was based on a criterion-referenced system where each level contains descriptors that can be related

Text Box 4.1

KS2/3 transition in science: a quiz

Please tick **one** box true or false for each statement (the ticks show the team's 'answers').

		True	False
(1)	Level 4 in Science at Key Stage 2 is the same as level 4 in Science at Key Stage 3.	✓	
(2)	Level 4 in Science Attainment Target 1 (Sc1) in Key Stage 2 is the same as level 4 in Sc1 at Key Stage 3.	✓	
(3)	National Curriculum Primary Science was introduced into all primary schools 8 years ago.		✓
(4)	Low-attaining pupils make the least progress in Key Stage 3.	✓	
(5)	Year 6 pupils can get a level 6 from their KS2 SATs.		✓
(6)	Children's attitude to science declines during Key Stage 3.	✓	
(7)	2 out of every 5 pupils fail to make the expected progress by the end of Key Stage 3.	✓	
(8)	At Key Stage 2 science teaching is more concerned with scientific enquiry than learning ideas and theories.	✓	
(9)	Science work should relate to real-life contexts at Key Stage 2. This is less important at Key Stage 3.		✓
(10)	Pupils are expected to draw line graphs by the end of Key Stage 2.	✓	

I think the most important reason why many children do not progress as expected in science in Key Stage 3 is:

Source: based on an idea in: DFES, 2002c.

Text Box 4.2

'Answers' to quiz questions on KS2/3 transfer in science

(1) **TRUE**. National Curriculum (NC) attainment levels are 'best fit' descriptions based on specific performance criteria that apply to any key stage. The argument against equivalence centres on the effects of change in context, teaching and methods of assessment used at different key stages.

(2) **TRUE**. As above. Similar differences of opinion apply but it is more likely that the complexity of context, the equipment and methods will affect pupils' performance.

(3) **FALSE**. It was introduced in 1989. The first pupils to transfer to KS3, having followed six years of primary science, did so in 1995.

(4) **TRUE**. One-third of pupils achieving level 3 at KS2 remain at the same level by the end of KS3.

(5) **FALSE**. KS2 pupils were able to take an extension paper for level 6. (This ceased in 2003.)

(6) **TRUE**. Current research shows that pupils' attitudes to science remain about the same in Y7 as they were in Y6. Attitudes decline by Y9. In English attitudes improve and in mathematics they go down following transfer.

(7) **TRUE**. Almost 90 per cent of pupils reach the expected target for science (level 4) at Key Stage 2 but about 70 per cent reach the target for Key Stage 3 (level 5). There have been slight improvements at Key Stage 3 since 2000.

(8) **TRUE**. A matter of opinion but the weighting for Sc1 is much higher at KS2 being 40 per cent of the whole assessment whereas as KS3 it represents only 25 per cent. Some might argue that Sc1 is fundamental to learning science and so should be equal in status at all key stages.

(9) **FALSE**. Open to opinion, but there is no reason why 'real-life' contexts should be less important to learning science at Key Stage 3 than they are at Key Stages 2 and 1. It is true that science ideas and theories get harder and more abstract in KS3 but that does not imply that the teaching should dissociate science from its applications. There is evidence that schools that place science teaching in its social, moral, cultural and spiritual settings improve pupils' motivation and attitudes to science.

> **(10) TRUE.** The expectation, for example, in the QCA scheme of work for science, is that most pupils should be able to do this by the end of KS2. The NC levels for science are more ambiguous as they seem to imply that only pupils performing at level 5 and above should be able to construct line graphs. Pupils' investigations often involve two continuous variables by the end of KS2 and so they should at least know that line graphs are the most appropriate means of displaying the findings in these cases.

to pupils' performance irrespective of their age. If we look at the report that guided the production of the first version of the National Curriculum for science in 1988 this seems a valid thing to do.

> Assessment, whether for feedback to pupils or overall reporting and monitoring ... should be criterion referenced. Given this, it follows that different pupils may satisfy a given criterion at different ages: to tie the criteria to particular ages would only risk either limiting the very able, or giving the least able no reward, or both. (DES/WO, 1988b: para. 99)

Specific criteria used to assess the National Curriculum in science have been subsumed into general level descriptions in different combinations over the years, but they are still essentially based on those that appeared in the first version in 1989. The question of how these criteria should be applied at different key stages has never been satisfactorily resolved and has, therefore, been open to interpretation. The fact that teachers from both phases in our study were about equally split on this issue reflects this uncertainty (about 50 per cent from each phase claimed statement 1 was false). The argument that levels can rarely be interpreted as the same in KS2 and KS3 and, therefore, that the statement is false, centres around differences in contexts of teaching and learning in which specific aspects of skills, knowledge and understanding have been assessed. It was our experience that some teachers argued, for example, that it is easier for a pupil to describe differences in properties of materials in terms of what is taught in programmes of study at Key Stage 2 than at Key Stage 3 because the expectation is that more abstract ideas, for example, in terms of the particle theory, should inform pupils' explanations. While we appreciate and can accept this, we believe, as the quote from the DfES training materials above stated, that such claims in these types of argument are a distraction. The key point, as well as one of the main messages of the book is, that unless secondary teachers are able to recognize and come to a better appreciation of the levels of skill, knowledge and understanding in science that many of their pupils arrive with from KS2, their pupils' progress will continue to be hampered.

We inserted another statement into the quiz about equivalence of levels (statement 2) to see if the same uncertainty might apply to the assessment of

Table 4.1   A comparison of teachers' responses to the statements in the quiz

		TRUE		FALSE	
Statements		**Primary teachers**	**Secondary teachers**	**Primary teachers**	**Secondary teachers**
1	Level 4 in Science at Key Stage 2 is the same as level 4 in science at Key Stage 3	**35 (49%)**	**36 (44%)**	36 (51%)	46 (56%)
2	Level 4 in Science Attainment Target 1 (Sc1) in Key Stage 2 is the same as level 4 in Sc1 at Key Stage 3	**44 (62%)**	**45 (55%)**	27 (38%)	37 (45%)
3	National Curriculum Primary Science was introduced into primary schools eight years ago	26 (37%)	37 (45%)	**44 (62%)**	42 (51%)
4	Low-attaining pupils make the least progress in Key Stage 3	**41 (58%)**	**39 (48%)**	30 (42%)	42 (51%)
5	Year 6 pupils can get a level 6 from their KS2 SATs	51 (72%)	42 (51%)	**19 (27%)**	38 (46%)
6	Children's attitude to science declines during Key Stage 3	**54 (76%)**	**69 (84%)**	17 (24%)	12 (15%)
7	Two out of every five pupils fail to make the expected progress by the end of Key Stage 3	**60 (85%)**	**68 (83%)**	10 (14%)	14 (17%)
8	At Key Stage 2 science teaching is more concerned with scientific enquiry than learning ideas and theories	**49 (69%)**	**41 (50%)**	22 (31%)	39 (48%)
9	Science work should relate to real-life contexts at Key Stage 2. This is less important at Key Stage 3	28 (39%)	6 (7%)	**42 (59%)**	**74 (90%)**
10	Pupils are expected to draw line graphs by the end of Key Stage 2	**58 (82%)**	**57 (70%)**	12 (17%)	21 (26%)

Notes: [Nil responses, of which there were very few, have not been included.
Primary teachers n = 71; secondary teachers n = 82]

process skills (scientific enquiry, or Sc1, as it is called in the National Curriculum). The results showed that more teachers in both phases and, slightly more primary teachers than secondary teachers, were inclined to accept equivalence of levels for Sc1 than they were for science as a whole. This fits with findings of other studies (Jarman, 1997; Peacock, 1999). In conferences and workshops, discussions on the issue of relative equivalence of levels in Sc1 were very revealing. Opinions spilt into two main camps.

1 Claims that levels of skills in scientific enquiry should be judged on their own merits as they represent the ways in which pupils have applied decisions and strategies to the task in hand, and this is independent of the context and conceptual demands of the task.
2 Claims that the context and procedural and conceptual demands of practical tasks inevitably change from KS2 to KS3, and therefore the interpretation of the ways in which skills are used and applied must also be different.

Again we had sympathy with both views, but decided that we would say the statement was true. In discussions with teachers we concentrated on the levels of procedural demand within tasks, while acknowledging that the context and conceptual demand of the work have an influence. Later, in describing the practical work involved in the two bridging units (see Chapter 6), we showed how the procedural demand of tasks was designed to progress so that pupils in Y7 would build on their previous work in Y6 but find new work in Y7 sufficiently challenging. This is a 'trick' that we thought designers of other bridging work in science had missed, and so the thinking embraced by these discussions was an essential part of our preparation. On reflection, these discussions were also important in persuading teachers using bridging units to adopt sufficient progression that recognized pupils' previous capabilities and learning.

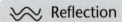 Reflection

To what extent should assessment of investigative (practical or process) skills recognize the contexts in which they have been assessed? How can teachers in Y7 be made more confident about the levels at which Y6 pupils have been assessed?

Differing emphasis in science teaching

We added statements (8) and (9) to the original quiz to explore different perspectives that primary and secondary teachers might have on the balance of enquiry-focused work, theoretical content and contexts for science work. This issue of the contexts for learning science emerged in discussions of pupils' voices in the previous chapter but the responses here shed a different light on the issue. If we take responses to the two statements (8 and 9) shown in Table 4.1 together there is an interesting pattern. Primary teachers' choices showed that they were much more likely to see secondary science as theoretically based and abstract than were secondary teachers, though statement 9 might have been rather ambiguous and would be better worded as 'Science work should be related more to real-life contexts at Key Stage 2 than it should be at Key Stage 3'. An interesting point to note here is that, in spite of the double question of statement 9, secondary teachers still opted overwhelmingly for the 'false' option. In other words secondary teachers were overwhelmingly convinced (90 per cent of them) that real-life contexts should be a strong feature of Key Stage 3 science.

We welcomed the result and were hopeful that it represented a desire to adopt context-led teaching particularly at Key Stage 3. It was reported in the last chapter that there is strong research evidence to support the use of real-life, industrial and commercial contexts, and particularly their value in improving pupils' motivation and their attitudes to science (Bennett et al., 2003). The Office for Standards in Education (Ofsted) has also found that context-led science is a key feature of effective science departments in secondary schools (Ofsted, 2002c). However, constraints due to high-stakes national testing and a curriculum over-filled with content at both key stages may have constrained these good intentions. A group of science educators gathered to consider the changes needed in Key Stage 3 science has recommended that:

> Young people ... need to engage with the scientific information they meet in everyday contexts ... A new curriculum at Key Stage 3 needs to ... engage with scientific issues that affect contemporary life, and to begin to consider the way science works, including the role of scientific evidence and the ethical and moral implication of certain choices. (Bennett et al., 2006: 5)

As discussed in the previous chapter, it is to be hoped that these recommendations will lead to a more contextualized and therefore more enjoyable experience of learning science, particularly at Key Stage 3.

Patterns in explanations for post-transfer regression

Since regression in KS3 is recognized as a key issue in KS2/3 transfer, and indeed the main reason why the project teams at York were engaged in trying to do something about it, it seemed sensible to include an opportunity in the 'quiz' for teachers to give their explanations for the phenomenon. Although a summary of reasons was provided in Chapter 2, the written responses provided to the open question at the end of the 'quiz' were much

Table 4.2 Most frequent reasons to explain post-transfer regression

Category	Sub-category	KS2 No. (%) of responses	KS3 No. (%) of responses
Social	Changes at puberty	4 (7%)	5 (7%)
Nature of teaching	Different teaching styles	0 (0%)	9 (13%)
	Teachers' expectations	0 (0%)	5 (7%)
	Uninspiring/boring teaching	1 (1%)	4 (6%)
Nature of work	More theoretical and abstract at KS3	4 (7%)	3 (4%)
	Less practical/skills at KS3	5 (9%)	2 (3%)
	KS2 work repeated	6 (11%)	19 (27%)
Pupils' attitudes and expectations	Complacency	4 (7%)	2 (3%)
	Less motivated	9 (13%)	4 (5%)
Assessment	Previous levels ignored	1 (2%)	12 (17%)

Notes: Primary teachers n = 54; secondary teachers n = 71

more varied than those collected through informal discussions at conferences. We coded over 40 sub-categories of response. The full list of codes and the frequencies of responses can be viewed on the project website at www.york.ac.uk/depts/educ/projs/STAY/pubandres.htm.

Table 4.2 summarizes the most frequent responses from primary and secondary teachers who completed this part of the quiz (there were 24 per cent and 13 per cent non-responses from primary and secondary teachers respectively – mainly in versions of the quiz completed and sent online via the AZSTT website).

In one sense, there was little that we had not expected from reading the research and from our own experiences. The fact that such a wide range of perceptions existed and how closely these related to those identified in the literature and research on transition was, on the one hand, a positive sign that teachers and others are aware of the difficulties that pupils face. On the other hand, we were concerned that there is so much awareness, yet little action to do much about some of these problems.

Perhaps one of the most striking features of the results is the number of secondary teachers who admitted that KS2 work is often repeated in KS3 (27 per cent). In contrast, primary teachers were hopeful that the work they had covered would not be repeated (11 per cent). Yet this still, means that over two-thirds of the secondary specialists surveyed either do not recognize this to be a problem, see plenty of other more important factors more likely to cause regression or who just do not care. Here are some typical responses that primary and secondary teachers provided about this issue (P=primary teacher, S = secondary teacher):

(Pupils regress) because work is often repeated in the initial stages of teaching at Key Stage 3 and children become bored easily and give up. They want to experience the things (equipment) they have not worked with at primary school. (P1)

KS3 teachers may not know what goes on at KS2 and may repeat topics. KS2 teachers may not know what goes on at KS3! Children's attitudes to science may decline towards the end of Y6 when there's lots of cramming of ideas and theories for the SATs. (P2)

Pupils have seen much of the KS3 context in KS2, especially the 'best' experiments. Main reason? Pressure to reach level 4/5 at KS2. (S1)

Recapping over work already done at KS2. Teachers having too low expectations of students coming into Year 7 therefore students not progressing in Year 7. (S2)

In response to S1, there is a claim that many of us have heard before – that primary schools 'pinch the best experiments' (that is, from those 'better' done at KS3). The teacher warrants the claim by asserting that it is pressure to push pupils to achieve at the highest levels that determines the experiments that are then 'stolen' from the adjoining key stage. The National Curriculum has never prescribed activities, methods or tasks to teach basic scientific principles at either key stage, though the use of schemes of work published by the government agency for curriculum and assessment (DfEE/QCA, 2000a; 2000b), commonly used by schools, should have avoided repetition of commonly used practical tasks. Ultimately, this remains one of the greatest challenges of primary–secondary transfer in science: how to provide science work in KS3, in contexts and topics and with apparatus and techniques that are familiar to pupils from their work in KS2, but that represent new and fresh challenges and build on what has been experienced before. Although the teams at York were principally engaged in designing bridging work for science, we have always taken the view that bridging work alone can only go so far in helping to address this issue. In Chapter 7 I discuss approaches that go beyond bridging in trying to avoid the repetition of whole chunks of practical work.

Before I leave discussion of data emerging from responses to the open question of the quiz, it is worth noting the number of secondary teachers (17 per cent) that felt KS2 attainment (as recognized by KS2 levels) is ignored. Only one primary teacher stated this. This is in stark contrast to the results discussed earlier for statements one and two of the 'quiz'.

Finally two very insightful comments, both provided by primary teachers, are worth considering.

Some of the concepts become more abstract and harder to grasp. The Sc1 skills are developed to make connections between all three sciences – at KS3 they become increasingly more separated so the full picture as taught in KS2 is not as obvious and can cause problems for less able pupils. (P3)

> As in all subjects, the children have worked through everything at least twice, done weeks of SAT revision, been assessed, tested, worked solidly and I believe they begin to suffer 'knowledge assimilation' fatigue. (P4)

I think the first of these alludes to a notion of relative integrity of the subject, especially when it comes to procedural knowledge. If pupils are taught by three (different) subject specialist teachers after transfer, as is often the case in English schools, then the internal integrity and continuity of science lessons that might have been present at KS2 is more difficult for the pupil to grasp – an interesting point. The second point is on something different – about assessment fatigue. This is a phenomenon that does not only apply at the Key Stage 2/3 boundary. It seems that England has the dubious reputation for having the greatest number of points of assessment across the ages of schooling, an issue I deal with in Chapter 7.

In the next two chapters actions to deal with post-transfer regression are explained and critiqued in some detail.

 ## Summary

The teacher voice includes suspicion that standards used to assess outcomes of learning science cannot be applied in the same ways either side of transfer. There is, however, some acceptance of equivalence for assessment of process skills. Teachers and others say they are keen to contextualize science at both sides of transfer, although research findings are less optimistic that this actually happens in practice. Secondary teachers are more likely to accept that repetition takes place, and sometimes blame this on experiments that might have been 'stolen' by primary teachers from those previously more suited to Key Stage 3.

Suggested actions

- Use the quiz provided in Text Box 4.1 to stimulate debate about the most important pedagogical issues facing teachers interested in developing better continuity and progression in science.
- Use the 'answers' provided as Text Box 4.2 to stimulate further discussions of the issues.
- Compare responses collected from the open question at the end of the quiz in Text Box 4.1 with the categories and frequencies of responses shown and discussed in this chapter.
- Use the activity suggested in Chapter 2 to identify practical tasks that might be used at each key stage and what might be done to avoid this.

5

Bridging the Divide: Part 1

Celia Moore

Chapter overview

The emotional, physical and environmental impacts of transfer are considered. Examples of how the five bridges – administrative, social, curriculum, pedagogic and metacognitive – are used to reduce social and learning 'shock' for pupils at transfer are provided. Solutions are not unique to learning science, though all impact on it.

Consider what it felt like for you when you started your present job. You might have moved from a different school or local authority, moved house, changed roles in the same school, been recruited following initial teacher training or from industry. You might also have left behind an established friendship group. As you presumably applied for a post you wanted, you may have felt quite pleased with your success at getting the job, excited even.

How did you then feel on day 1 in your new job? Did you know exactly what to do, what the routines were, which car parking space not to use? Did you know your way around the school or were you limited to a single route between staffroom and teaching base? Staff in some schools may never be truly conversant with their campus, particularly as there are now fewer requirements to cover for absent colleagues who teach in other locations on campus. How long was it before you felt settled, had established yourself in whatever social scene or community was to your liking and felt able to challenge some of the policy directives coming your way?

As an adult you have had years of experience of being in new situations, and your new job was of your own choice and making. For our young people school transfers have been foisted on them at arbitrary times in their social and cognitive development, suiting some individuals better than others. Some will have had little choice about which school they moved to, either because their parents made the decision or as the result of parents not being successful in their first choice of school in the application process (see Glossary under 'Admissions'). Induction days (see later) are important events in schools' calendars, yet some pupils might have missed these if parents chose the post-SATs period to take family holidays. In the UK, advantageous holiday prices in school terms can be very tempting. I am not sure, however, how many parents realize the folly of their actions and implications for their children post-transfer. Combine all these factors with the aching desire of the child to be elsewhere, and the immediate future does not look good.

Change is constant in our fast-moving society. Children and young people are not exempt from this, nor should they be. The difficulty arises for them when the change is system driven; done to them and for them, rather than with them. Stepping into the unknown can result in anxiety, so having the skills to deal with it is important. On the other hand, developing a process so smooth and slick that pupils hardly notice the change is both unlikely and undesirable as 'learned helplessness' would then become the order of the day, presenting different problems that would probably result in poor progress.

Every child really does matter (especially at transfer)

It is well established that pupils need to be in an appropriate state to enable effective learning. Their emotional health and well-being, physical health and safety must all be taken into account (Corrie, 2003; Curran, 2006; Goleman, 1996; Jensen, 1995). This is the cornerstone of legislation called Every Child Matters, introduced for schools in England and Wales by the Children Act 2004 (www.opsi.gov.uk/acts2004). Changes resulting from this legislation are having a significant impact on transfer policies and practices in English schools.

Abraham Maslow's 'hierarchy of need' demonstrates clearly that for anyone to achieve their potential there is a plethora of personal needs that must be met: food, water, shelter and physical safety are paramount (Maslow, 1987). Indeed these can be recognized as *building blocks* supporting higher level development. It is only when these are in place that love, emotional security and knowing that you belong become significant. These in turn support the development of *self-esteem, positive learning, engagement* and *personal success*. Few people start along their developmental pathways with a desire to limit personal successes, neither do parents and teachers have underachievement as a desired outcome for their pupils. Unfortunately, as was discussed in Chapter 2, underachievement is a reality for many of our learners following transfer from primary to secondary schools. This is what one well-known report had to say about lack of post-transfer progress in science: 'transfer under present conditions results in up to two out of every five pupils failing to make expected progress during the year immediately following the change of school' (Galton et al., 1999: 10).

Maslow's building blocks – nourishment, personal safety, love, affection and belonging – support the development of self-esteem, a higher-level function that enables personal fulfilment. These are, however, transient and as surely as someone can climb the pyramid, they can slip back down again.

Take as an example a Y7 pupil, David, who has moved to secondary school with several other pupils from his old school. There are several of these pupils in the same tutor group and so friendships continue. The first few days in school are fine and all are settling into new routines. The pupils are then put into different sets for science, not David's favourite subject. In his new set there is no one he was at primary school with and he feels isolated and vulnerable. David is not feeling emotionally secure and he does not feel part of the group, all the others know someone else. He feels isolated and that he does not belong. This is not conducive to his learning. David has slipped down Maslow's pyramid and is further away from being able to develop self-esteem and achieve self-actualization. He needs to establish camaraderie with his fellow students before he will be able to give all his attention to learning something that he knows he struggles with. It is difficult to understand how young people would be in a position to enjoy, engage and achieve, if they are feeling personally, socially or emotionally vulnerable.

There will be many reasons for this vulnerability. Some are difficult for the class teacher to have an impact on; others are well within their professional remit. Dealing with pupils' learning difficulties and their dispositions are absolutely the responsibility of each and every teacher. A pupil or student in a dishevelled or angry state because of a difficult situation at home is an entirely different matter, often beyond that which the teacher can resolve. However, and this is the fundamental point, each fragile individual still needs to be included in the learning experience and recognized as a valuable part of the learning community. It is crucial that they are cared for, and cared about, if there really is a seriousness that, as new initiatives would claim, 'every child does indeed matter'. It is paramount, therefore, that teachers have a full understanding of the needs of young people, knowledge of their development and awareness of the impact that personal problems have on learning.

The work of Abraham Maslow gives us an accessible structure to understand pupils' needs in terms of development of their learning. However, we must also remember that pupils at the primary–secondary transfer are adolescents facing the inevitable changes of body and emotions and each will react differently. In 2003, The Trust for the Study of Adolescence reported that transition from primary to secondary school is a key time for young people and if the experience is not a good one it is likely to result in inappropriate risk-taking and exclusion later in school (Roker and Shepard, 2003). Studies in the USA concur that bad experiences at transfers are one of the most likely causes of high school failure (Roderick and Camburn, 1999).

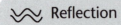

Reflection

What can be done in science departments to ensure that the personal and social well-being of new entrants, according to Maslow's building blocks, is catered for?

The administrative bridge

In Chapter 2, four common actions to smooth transfers and transitions were listed (Table 2.3). They are frequently mentioned by Maurice Galton and his co-workers at Cambridge, and are often referred to as the *four bridges* (Galton et al., 1999). In his later work, Galton added a fifth bridge concerned with 'learning to learn'. This is discussed at the end of the chapter, but first to administrative matters, Galton's first bridge.

The *administrative bridge* is crucial in all transfers. How could secondary schools be expected to welcome pupils if basics such as names and addresses are not available? I remember when I was about to go to secondary school there was a dispute between my mother and my primary school head teacher as to which secondary school I should attend. This was before the days of admissions and appeals procedures and so I was merely sent to a school of my mother's choosing. When I arrived there I was not expected and the school, knowing nothing about me, put me in the lowest ability class. That I had passed my eleven-plus examination (see Glossary) was irrelevant. At its most fundamental then, the administrative bridge facilitates transfer of essential pupil details from one school to another.

However, there is much more to this bridge. As we have learned in previous chapters, pupils arrive at secondary school not as 'clean goods' with untouched minds, but as having learned a great deal in their primary schools. Knowing what this is, how well it has been learned, and so giving knowledge and skill proper value is an important aspect of the administrative bridge and a key theme of this book. A 'clean slate' approach that allows teachers to disenfranchise pupils from prior learning, teach all learners from the same starting point and plod through the syllabus in a linear, stepped approach is much less common than it once was, and for that we should be grateful. As discussed in Chapter 3, however, there are many teachers in science departments who do not see it this way.

In order to enable differentiated teaching, schools have to know what has gone before, and Key Stage 2 SAT results can play a central role. However, SAT results do not provide the full picture; they are merely brush strokes on the transfer canvas. Many schools wish to avail themselves of much more than this and so request raw scores from end of key stage tests. Likewise, teacher assessments (TAs) may be part of data that follow a young person from one institution to the next. Local authorities play an important role, creating an infrastructure enabling schools to access much of the data by electronic means. This allows teachers in secondary schools to make effective use of data to plan for their new intake of pupils in plenty of time before they arrive.

There is another set of data, or more properly information, that should accompany an individual on their learning journey: details about the person themselves. Receiving teachers need to know if a child has free school meals, a medical condition or learning difficulty. They also need to know if attendance and punctuality have been concerns during the primary years. Schools that really are concerned about their pupils and believe in the values and principles of Every Child Matters, rather than attending merely to its rhetoric, will want much more. Knowing about sporting ability, musical talent, leadership qualities, difficult personal circumstances, and friendships begins to draw humanity out of the numbers and background statistics. Every pupil entering secondary school comes with a complex of thoughts, feelings and behaviours that makes each of them unique. It is the role of the secondary school to ensure that the individual flourishes, in the words of Marland and Rogers (1997: 1), 'to enable the child to become a student and more fully a person'. The administrative bridge facilitates this.

I would go further and suggest that best practice dictates that each pupil in each primary school should have a conversation with a significant member of staff from the school to which they will transfer. This enables the young person to feel valued, provides opportunities to ask about issues in private but, perhaps most importantly, pupils begin to develop a relationship with someone who will be a part of their future learning lives. It is difficult to overstate the importance of this to the young person. I am frequently amazed by the 20-year-olds who stop me on the streets of my home town telling me how much my Y6 visit meant to them and how important this was for them at that time in their lives.

These meetings, between secondary staff and future pupils, can be very productive if preparatory work is undertaken by staff on both sides of the transfer. The family of schools should agree jointly what information would be useful to the receiving school. A mechanism to maximize efficiency of collection and effectiveness of dissemination is essential. The spreadsheet shown as Figure 5.1 is an example and has been developed by various practitioners in Suffolk schools over a number of years.

Succinct comments can be written in the cells to inform secondary colleagues. For some headings, a colour-coding shortcut can be used: red to note a significant concern, amber if concerns arise on occasions and green if there are no problems at all. The colours will need to be assigned a number if data are to be sorted by computer. The spreadsheet note facility can then be used to provide additional inputs for any cell, and school-specific headings, tutor groups and subject sets added at the appropriate times. It then becomes a simple data sort to provide secondary colleagues with pupil-specific information at individual and group level. The spreadsheet can also become a vehicle for reporting progress of new secondary cohorts back to the feeder primary schools to engender collective interest in, and responsibility for, the learner journey. Using this information effectively to

Christian Name	Surname	Gender	School	10+ Reading	Teacher Ass			SEN	Attendance	Free Meal	Medical Issues	Physical Difficulties	Musical	Sporting	G & T	EAL
					En	Ma	Sc	A/A+/S	Good							
									Concern							
									Poor							
										Y	Y	Y	Y	Y	Y	Y

Notes:

10+ Reading: This is based on the Suffolk Reading test taken by many pupils in England at ages 8+, 10+ and 12+

Teacher Ass: Teacher Assessment is made by all teachers on Year 6 pupils in each of the core subjects. Secondary schools often use these for planning purposes before SATs results are available (see Glossary).

SEN (A/A + /S): Pupils with Special Educational Needs (SEN) are placed at different levels on the schools' Special Needs Register. This gives an indication of the extra help they can expect to receive. A– is used on the register to make staff aware of difficulties and any specific concerns. A+ indicates pupils will have an Individual Education Plan which states precisely the nature of the difficulties, and teaching strategies that should be employed. A– pupils with a Statement of Special Education Needs will have significant difficulties and it is a legal requirement that they receive the support detailed on their statement. This might include extra support from a teaching assistant.

Sporting: Pupils with significant talents in physical or sporting activities.

G&T: Pupils who are deemed to be academically gifted or talented in sports or performing arts. These pupils need to be identified in order that sufficient stretch and challenge is provided to engage them.

EAL: Pupils for whom English is an Additional Language, that is, not their mother tongue.

Figure 5.1 A portion of a spreadsheet used to transfer pupils' information from primary to secondary schools

enhance learning presents the biggest challenge, merely collecting data is not enough.

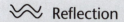

Reflection

As a receiving teacher, what information about pupils' learning would you need to provide for differentiated learning in science? In what form should this information be transferred?

Building social bridges

Policy issues

Galton et al. (1999) see the *social bridge* as alleviating the anxieties pupils might have about moving to a bigger school. Indeed, it seems that the anxieties of most pupils disappear quite quickly following transfer. This does not, however, prevent these anxieties from being there in the first place. For the minority of pupils that remain apprehensive, knowing that everyone else has settled in well does little to help, indeed it can increase individuals' concerns about their personal circumstances. The social bridge is about developing productive relationships between the receiving school and parents and carers, a laudable cause.

Many schools have programmes in place that have, as their main intention, easing the transfer process by making pupils feel comfortable in their new surroundings. Brighouse and Woods (2006) relate success in such endeavours to the context and cultures of schools and particularly to their leadership. Contexts and cultures, both movable feasts, need to be at the forefront of planning for each new cohort of incoming pupils. Each year group will be different and should be considered afresh. This does not mean starting transfer policy from scratch each year; rather, that the specific needs of the incoming group become the most important part of the context that drives policy and practice.

During the past decade much has been written about *emotional health* and well-being and its importance to all of us. These are, quite rightly, integral to the Every Child Matters agenda. They are also foci within a programme called *Social and Emotional Aspects of Learning* (SEAL). The programme has been used by primary schools since 2005 and is intended to develop social, emotional and behavioural skills for all pupils. There are five basic elements: self-awareness, motivation, managing feelings, empathy and social skills. Details of the programme can be found at www.standards.dfes.gov.uk/primary/publications/banda/seal.

The SEAL programme recognizes the intrapersonal as well as interpersonal aspects of learning and behaviour essential to facilitate 'personal growth' and the 'self-actualization' that Maslow brought to the fore. The programme was piloted in secondary schools from September 2007 and resources have been specifically written for schools to use either side of transfer. It is debatable just how much the secondary school science teacher knows about SEAL and its implications for their classrooms, but the programme offers significant opportunities. Science teachers use group work as a standard part of their practice. On many occasions, however, pupils are merely working in close proximity to each other rather than collaboratively. As part of the primary SEAL programme 'New beginnings' pupils have developed their social skills and by the end of Y6 will know how to work in groups and how to include others (DfES, 2005). They will have worked on 'Making choices' and 'Rights and responsibilities'. If a science teacher in the secondary school now develops group work based on what pupils have previously done, it is likely that their group work skills will be more effective than has previously been the case.

 Reflection

What are the positive gains of using collaborative group work in science lessons? Should more opportunities for group work be provided in Y7?

According to Galton et al. (1999) *induction days, open evenings* and special visits focusing on specific areas of the curriculum are particularly successful at easing these concerns discussed so far.

Open evenings

Open evenings are traditionally held in the autumn term to allow pupils and their caregivers the opportunity to look around the school, ask questions and form an opinion about joining a school. As part of the social bridge this is an opportunity for pupils to become familiar with the school and address anxieties. From the school's point of view the open evening is more of a public relations exercise aimed at recruiting sufficient pupil numbers to fill rolls and maximize funding. Schools put on excellent performances of their innovative, participative curriculum, and science departments are particularly good at this. Prospective pupils participate in exciting hands-on, practical activities, getting involved in 'real' science (as they often perceive it). They may have followed a forensic trail, looked at samples of cells or blood under microscopes, analysed ink on handwritten notes, coming to conclusions about who committed a dastardly crime. They will have been intrinsically motivated to engage fully with tasks, ably assisted by a plethora of helpful teachers, technicians and friendly pupils, all eager to give a good impression of school science. Significantly, they will not have had to produce any writing about these experiences.

At one visit to an open evening in autumn 2007, I saw pupils demon-strating heart dissection and lung function using real organs and checking DNA samples with sophisticated electrophoresis equipment. That was just in the biology department! In physics they had more 'toys' on display than you could shake a stick at and chemistry performed likewise – all whizzes and bangs. I find this is the norm for open evenings in many high schools I visit. It does, however, create an impression that each and every science lesson will present something interesting, exciting and new. The pupils will have had fun, parents will have been impressed and the school will have gone a long way towards recruiting a pupil, a serious issue in times of increasing parental choice of schools.

Induction days

Another standard part of the transfer package is the induction day, transfer day or junior six (J6) day, call it what you will. The aim of these days is to try out the school and become familiar with it prior to moving. While the aim is a noble one, I wonder if it is also misguided, or like open evenings, used in a misguided way. By the time July of Y6 comes around, decisions have already been made as to which school the pupils will attend, except for unfortunate individuals still engaged with appeals. Therefore this day is clearly not about recruitment, it is about sampling the school in order to (hopefully) relieve some of the quite natural anxieties that youngsters might be feeling. Again the pupils will be welcomed with open arms. The head teacher will greet them with a smile, a special programme of lessons will have been arranged, guides will ensure pupils do not get lost and a specially arranged lunchtime ensures the passage through the canteen is less trau-matic than it otherwise might be.

Consider for a moment whether this is a typical day youngsters will experience in September after they have transferred, or has it been dressed up for the occasion, setting false expectations? Teachers naturally want youngsters to have a good time and lessons will be well planned with lots of activities using teaching methods that appeal to and include all. There will be fewer pupils on site as Y11 and Y13 have left, Y12 will be ensconced in the sixth form and Y10 may be on work experience. With the campus quieter than usual, it is easier for staff to give their full attention to Y6 pupils. At the end of the day the majority of pupils report excellent experiences to their parents and carers. Teachers talk about having high expectations of pupils in order that stretch and challenge are to the fore. Perhaps there is a need to consider what the pupils expect to get out of the school experience. As far as science is concerned, this was discussed earlier in Chapter 3 outlining pupils' voices. Expectations of exciting science les-sons using specialist equipment, pupil-friendly pedagogy and lack of writ-ing can be quickly dashed if sitting in rows, watching demonstrations and extended writing are significant experiences, endemic in most lessons. Surely in these circumstances the pupil could be forgiven for feeling somewhat duped and therefore less committed to science than the school anticipated, having gone to great lengths to welcome them.

In many schools the first day of the September term might also be contrived to ease transfer. In many schools it is common practice for only Y7 and Y12 to attend school for the first few days and lessons for new entrants get under way gently after the first part of the day is spent with their form tutor. While this practice is to be applauded, I wonder how teachers perceive this use of their time. Time frequently is spent issuing timetables, considering significant school rules and taking part in 'ice-breaker' activities that encourage pupils to get to know each other. However, if the intent of such sessions remains merely at a level of socializing pupils, the real significance of transfer and transition, being about change, is lost.

 Reflection

How can open and induction days be made exciting without creating an artificial view of what science lessons will be like?

Peer mentoring

An important part of the social bridge is ways in which older pupils can be used to help new entrants settle. Helping new pupils understand and make sense of the ethos, culture and environment of the school are prerequisites to being in an emotionally appropriate state that enables effective learning to take place. The work of eminent psychologist Csikszentmihalyi (cited by Jenson, 1995) and Gilbert (2005) acknowledges that a 'state of flow' is an optimal internal state for learning. This is probably best explained as when you are so engrossed in your learning that time passes easily and on-task behaviour is the norm. This is achieved when high challenge is accompanied by low stress. In the preface to this book we told the story of Amin and Lisa and the emails they sent back to their primary schools as they experienced their first few weeks in their new secondary school. Consider what might also have happened to Lisa and Amin on just one day. Although I have adapted the story and my reflections on it for Amin and Lisa's case, it is based on a real experience I had as a teacher – one that had a lasting impact on my attitudes to pupils arriving in my school.

It is break time, the science prep room is full and it is the first week of term. A knock is heard on the door and some heads turn towards it as it opens. Surprisingly, Amin and Lisa walk in. They announce they are there to collect some beakers but they do not get more than two steps into the room before a member of staff yells at them, and I do mean *yells*, about their lack of rights to be in the prep room and that they should know better.

After that experience and for some time after, every time Amin and Lisa met a science teacher this was accompanied by high stress, flooding their amygdylas with flight and fear responses, and leaving them in no fit state to learn. As a teacher, I was left wondering why these two children should have expected to know the particular entry protocols of the science prep room. You see, in Year 6, Amin and Lisa had been trusted custodians in their respective primary schools, making the staff tea, delivering it to the playground and washing the mugs afterwards. They were regular visitors to staffrooms in their schools for all manner of reasons. Their schools had no strict rules or protocols forbidding them entering such places. So I came to the conclusion that it is incumbent on teachers to know much more about the preceding key stage, but beyond mere curriculum knowledge, to therefore take account of the full pupil experience.

Fortunately many schools do recognize transfers as much more than the physical moves between institutions and consider the emotional well-being of their pupils. Older pupils can be trained as *peer mentors*, providing a support service from the informed stance of pupil-as-expert. Training for mentors is important and encourages them to revisit thoughts, feelings and anxieties about their own transfers to secondary school. They will be trained to listen to younger pupils and show empathy. They are a sounding board and safety net. New pupils are often happier talking to peers about their problems than to adults. They can feel unsure about approaching teachers, particularly as they have been repeatedly told that secondary school is about growing up, having more responsibility and independence. In addition, the organizational system of most secondary schools does not foster the kind of relationships they have been used to with their Y6 teacher. Peer mentors champion pupils' self-efficacy within a supported learning community (Cowie and Wallace, 2000). They can be a crutch for many young people and can stop small concerns escalating into major problems. Their role in enabling an appropriate state for learning is clear.

In one school I worked in, Y12 and Y13 were trained to support pupils in lessons, and science benefited from this. Those choosing to support in this way were studying for AS and A2 science examinations and therefore well placed to help youngsters with their learning. Pupils were able to access more guidance than would usually be available to them, mentors developed their own skills and the relationship between pupil and mentor supported Y7 learners in more than just science lessons.

Curriculum bridges

In theory there should be no need for curriculum bridges in UK schools as that is what a National Curriculum from Foundation Stage (ages 3–5) to Y11 (age 16) should have provided. However, schools are autonomous institutions overlaying their own interpretations on curriculum legislation.

Also important is the number of schools feeding secondaries. It is a reality that many larger secondary schools work with 30 or more feeder primary schools. These primary schools will have taught the science curriculum in a variety of ways, using different resources. The Y7 science teacher is faced with trying to create homogeneity from all this disparity of experience.

As we saw in Chapters 2 and 3, Galton et al. (1999) were clear that by the end of Y7 pupils find school a less enjoyable experience than they had in their primary schools. Science is a particular concern when pupils now spend much of their time copying notes or writing instructions, with the teacher leading most activities. Gone then are some of the exciting, innovative practices they had been lured with in open and induction days. This is compounded by having fewer pupil–teacher discussions, an important way of developing relationships. It is easy to see why pupils remember their primary school days with fond affection. Secure long-term relationships, less emphasis on extended writing; things could hardly have been better. Through this rose-tinted hue pupils may forget that much of their final year was given to preparation and revision for SATs. This is a quote from one Y6 teacher justifying revision for science SATs:

> In the beginning of the Spring term, one of the afternoon lessons every week is a science revision period because (a) I'm a scientist and (b) I recognize that this is the only fact learning subject they're tested on at the end of Key Stage 2 and they have to remember four years' worth of facts ...
> (Galton et al. 1999: 16)

Galton et al. go on to quote head teachers who admit to revision and booster class drudgery in Y6. Few pretend it is best practice but see it as inevitable if their pupils and schools are to be deemed successful. Schools endeavour to present SATs positively to pupils, parents and carers. It may be, therefore, that pupils view SATs as a necessary evil, one which once out of the way will present opportunities for all manner of reverie in the run-up to transfer. In the worst-case scenarios it is possible that no new or significant learning has taken place in the post-SATs period, that is, for a full three months preceding transfer. Pupils may then be out of the *habit of learning*.

As discussed in Chapter 2, a spiral curriculum means visiting content and concept areas on several occasions and at different key stages. At each stage more complex knowledge is presented requiring greater understanding. As we have seen from research, pupils' perceptions are that they have done topics before and either know all about it, or could not understand it then and this time it is likely to be no different or even worse. If this is the attitude then learners of all abilities quickly disengage. For example pupils do not really understand the difference between naming the parts of a buttercup at Key Stage 3 and what was expected from a similar activity at Key Stage 1. As far as pupils are concerned they are just repeating work. It is interesting to note that I have yet to see this particular topic being used on transfer or induction days. Teachers seem to know pupils have done it before and will do it again, probably twice.

Schools cannot be held responsible for the content of the science curriculum they are required to teach. However, it is beholden on each department to understand what has gone before and acknowledge prior learning. Consider how easily you switch off when a friend or colleague is relating a fairly involved anecdote you have heard before; even worse if you were not interested first time around. It is crucial to ensure that learners know what is new in what is being taught and that teachers are aware of what has already been covered. In the next two chapters bridging work and science enquiry tasks that were designed to address these problems are described.

Combining *social* and *curriculum* bridges seems worthwhile. The power of both in smoothing transfers would be good to realize. In one school, a cross-curricular project involving science and geography departments produced work based on Inuit life, food chains and global warming. Primary pupils were encouraged to work creatively, developing presentations to show to secondary teachers. These experiences were augmented through learning Inuit words in the modern foreign languages department of the secondary school. Pupils worked with teachers from different faculties in the secondary school in a manner that they were used to and in the familiar surroundings of their primary classrooms. From the teachers' perspectives, the opportunity to meet with several colleagues from each phase for planning and delivery resulted in further cross-phase initiatives. This school has also hosted active learning evenings to engage parents in the curriculum early in Y7, a significant success for a school that previously struggled to get parents to attend anything.

In Welsh schools, cross-phase professional development has been common, with corresponding shared understanding of the curriculum either side of transfer. One school in South Wales chose to develop a passport to encourage pupils to achieve 'Citizen of the School Status'. Passport stamps were collected by pupils for activities such as raising money for charity, participating in choir and good work in subjects including science. The process began on transfer day and concluded with a high-profile speaker presenting passports to participating pupils at a special ceremony. The passport idea has been used to improve the quality of information transferred from primary to secondary schools in science. This is described in Chapter 8.

Building pedagogic bridges

Teaching, and so pedagogy, is often very different either side of the transfer. In primary schools whole-class teaching, discussion and active learning opportunities abound. Extended writing, individual performance and limited discussion is more the case in secondary schools. This can be a shock for pupils. There is also a significant subject specialist approach in secondary schools, which is not often the case in the primary phase.

At transfer it is important to prepare pupils for differences they will encounter. One of the biggest is the number of teachers young people will work with. In Y6 pupils might be taught by a maximum of three teachers. In Y7 it is common for Y7 pupils to work with 12 or more teachers. Many pupils have to contend with more than this if the timetabler has dictated they will be taught by two or more teachers for some subjects. If science is organized as biology, physics and chemistry, this means three science teachers are experienced in one week. This is before teachers are substituted to attend Inset or if they are absent through illness. That is a lot of different personalities, with different teaching styles, for an 11-year-old to come to terms with. In one school, for a variety of reasons, one Y7 science class had been taught by eight different science teachers by Easter. This is not really a sound foundation on which to build relationships with teacher or subject. It does not make pupils feel valued and certainly does nothing for continuity and progression. I am left wondering who will remember this at Y11 when some of these pupils do not achieve the science results that their general ability seemed to predict.

To take account of good primary pedagogical practice an increasing number of secondary schools are employing primary-trained teachers to act as champions. When schools have embraced this philosophy they are likely to make considerable demands on *how* colleagues teach as well as *what* they teach. For example, in science primary pupils are used to working in groups to gather equipment and design a fair test having been set a problem by the teacher. Their learning will be active with much discussion and negotiation. Creativity and curiosity are to the fore. Results will often be recorded in diagrammatic form, with pupils being given the opportunity to present their findings to the teacher or class. Careful questioning clarifies understanding and extends thinking. It is also inclusive of those individuals who are not adept at writing up their findings. How different from secondary science when the teacher demonstrates an experiment, all pupils try to replicate it and the results are written up in individual exercise books to be marked in privacy by the teacher. Primary pedagogy has much to offer the secondary teacher.

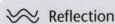 **Reflection**

What pedagogical practices should be continued from primary school into secondary school lessons?

The new bridge – 'learning to learn'

Galton added a fifth bridge to his original set, recognizing that a few schools were more interested in pursuing generalizable cognitive gains than in building subject bridges. Enabling pupils to take responsibility for their own learning, becoming professional pupils and knowing how they learn are the significant elements of this bridge (Galton et al., 2003b). It should be recognized, however, that as with the pedagogical bridge these are paid less attention at transfer because they are difficult to deliver. Yet perhaps they have more to offer in terms of taking learning forward and tackling the post-transfer performance 'dip'.

Some schools have paid heed to this area, creating induction programmes more extensive in their remit than those usually on offer. They look at induction over a period of time in much the same way that a new teacher joining the staff of a school would have. If induction is important for professional adults, why not for pupils? But induction must not be a token gesture or pupils will be further marginalized. In one school pupils concentrated on personal skills of collaboration and working in a new environment. Science teachers identified an aspect of the curriculum, for example, the Earth and space, for pupils to work on together. This involved the need for research, presentation, notation, critical thinking, teamwork and decision-making. Pupils were engaged, through peer tutoring and group work as they strove to impress their new teachers. Relationships, which are the foundation of mutual respect, were developed more naturally as teachers and pupils worked alongside each other. This was much more productive than drawing another poster about the Bunsen burner or copying laboratory and safety rules.

Another school, recognizing that anxiety and information overload gets in the way of learning, developed a comprehensive induction programme. Time was spent with the tutor developing class relationships and considering personal learning styles. Pupils were then taught about brain function, how to nurture their brain and how knowing your learning style can be important to you. For the next three weeks all Y7 pupils worked in their tutor groups on a project called 'Medieval Realms' (the school has Humanities Specialist School Status). The project was taken on board in all subjects and teachers used interactive learning activities, developing an *Assessment for Learning* and *Learning to Learn* approach (see the Glossary for definitions). A visit to a nearby castle provided an additional bonding opportunity, early in the school year. Parents were invited to a plenary session at the end of the three-week project at which pupils had a 'show and tell' session about learning in their new school. Among other things, pupils demonstrated fire extinguishers and battering rams that had been made in science. They had to conduct rigorous research about material available in medieval times and appropriate designs. It is unquestionable that significant learning took place. During this time pupils were given no homework and no timetable.

Conclusion

At the start of secondary school the majority of young people have new friendship groups and pecking orders uppermost in their minds. Learning is merely a sideshow. If youngsters can be well prepared, engaged in creating the learning and valued for who they are and what they have already done, they are much more likely to achieve their potential.

Some pupils find moving schools a traumatic experience. Underachievement is a real possibility. If the situation is unresolved they are at risk of further alienation. Redirecting the social bridge to become an overarching umbrella that reaches into all the other bridges and giving it the function of overseeing emotional well-being would open up policy thinking to look beyond friendship groups and anti-bullying policies. Considering transfer policy in this light, as an all embracing agency, overseen by the emotional well-being umbrella and encompassing the nuances of all five bridges, would bring greater coherence. It would promote personal development as being at the heart of learning as the new secondary curriculum, to be introduced in England in 2008, would seem to be about. School improvement would undoubtedly follow if all pupils engaged with their learning having achieved the appropriate internal state bolstered by an external environment more appropriate to their needs.

Nicholls and Gardner (1999) warn that getting induction right could be the pivotal action that promotes success for pupils in the secondary system. Transfer, transition and induction programmes should be about preparing pupils to be ready for learning in new environments. This is an ongoing process, not just a quick fix on one day or one week. Transition is the glue of the learning journey. Ask yourself this question: is it flour and water paste or superglue in your school?

Summary

Transition between schools is complex and impacts on individuals in different ways. Schools, parents and local authorities all have a part to play in ensuring that negative impact is reduced. Emotional well-being of pupils is a crucial aspect of transition, which acts as an umbrella for all other bridges.

Suggestions for action

- Primary and secondary staff should engage in dialogue about content of learning and pedagogical practices to ensure continuity and progression.
- Secondary staff should know about the pupils as individuals prior to transition.
- Schools have to take the anxieties of pupils at transition seriously, no matter how transient these may be.
- Recognize the importance of pupils' emotional health and well-being at this significant life change.

6

Bridging the Divide:
Part 2 – Science Bridging Units

Chapter overview

The rationale and key design features of bridging units produced by the York STAY project team are considered. Contexts for lessons and how to provide the right degree of continuity and progression through development of teaching and suitable learning tasks are discussed. Examples of teaching and learning resources from the bridging units are provided. The evaluation of bridging work challenges criticisms of this type of work.

The range of strategies used by schools to address curricular and pedagogical discontinuities, Galton's third and fourth bridges, include co-observations of teaching, improving teachers' knowledge of content taught each side of transfer, shared assessment of pupils' work and jointly planned teaching. It is on this last area that much recent attention and effort has been focused in the UK and other countries. A common approach is to plan work that pupils start at the end of primary school and continue and complete when they arrive in secondary school. Schemes in this area are variously described as transition units (DfES, 2002a), link projects (Davies and McMahon, 2004) and bridging units (Braund, 2002; QCA, 2000). As with other actions on transfer, work has been most prolific in English and mathematics where units of work have been made available to schools in England by the Qualifications and Curriculum Authority (QCA, 2000) and the Department for Education and Skills (DfES, 2002a; 2003). More recently these organizations have also provided materials in non-core subjects, geography, music and ICT. In science no such units were available nationally and so it was left to groups of schools, often working in conjunction with local authorities and/or in collaboration with higher education institutions (HEIs), to devise these materials.

Rationale and design

The aims for bridging in science are consistent with those for mathematics and English described in guidance produced by the DfES:

> Bridging units should ensure that:
>
> - Pupils experience a lesson structure they are familiar with and understand.
> - There is a consistency in teaching approach that helps pupils respond to new people (that is, classmates and new teachers) in new surroundings.
> - Pupils build on their early successes and demonstrate what they know, understand and can do in the context of the work they did in Year 6.
> - Teachers are better informed about pupils' strengths and weaknesses and can use the lessons to confirm their assessments and plan teaching programmes that meet the needs of their pupils.
> - There is greater continuity and progression and less repetition of work. (DfES, 2002a: 3)

Units designed by the STAY project team at York focused on the scientific enquiry (Sc1) area of the National Curriculum in England (DfEE/QCA, 1999) and particularly on the *considering and evaluating evidence* strand. This decision was taken for two main reasons:

1 As experienced in other attempts at bridging in science, it proved difficult to agree on a content area (topic) that all primary and secondary schools could teach at the end of Y6 and again at the start of Y7. Scientific enquiry was seen by the York team as central to science learning and as a consistent element present on either side of transfer, whatever topic is taught.

2 The strand of scientific enquiry (Sc1) called *considering and evaluating evidence* in the National Curriculum for England and Wales (DfEE, 1999) was given an increased emphasis in the version published in 1999 and was seen as an area in which teachers would appreciate activities to use with pupils and support for and advice on their teaching. This is still the case (though it is part of what is now called 'How science works').

In this chapter, bridging units designed by the STAY team at York are considered against key design features and the reasons why these were thought important. These features draw heavily on the research evidence presented in previous chapters. Thus the STAY bridging units can truly claim to be an example of research-informed practice.

Duration and organization

The STAY team produced two bridging units, one called Fizzy Drinks and the other called Bread, each representing about six hours of teaching in Y6 and four hours of teaching in Y7. Teaching time in each unit was limited for two main reasons. First, previous experiences in Australia (Scharf and Schibeci, 1990) and in Scotland (Dutch and McCall, 1974) showed that lengthy bridging projects have a negative impact on pupils' attitudes at transfer. In Australia this was particularly true for low-achieving girls who ended up showing marked declines in attitudes compared with similar pupils who had not been involved in bridging work. Second, Y6 teachers have a packed timetable of activities they wish to pursue in the weeks following national tests (Galton et al., 2003c). Although suggested teaching time was limited, many schools using STAY units went beyond this as pupils seemed to become so absorbed in their work. In primary schools we found the commonest organization was to teach one or two STAY lessons each week over a maximum six-week period following the completion of national tests in late May. A few primary schools held a special 'science week' in which the lessons were taught as a block. In secondary schools STAY lessons were most commonly taught alongside other work, as a discrete two-week module at the start of the year or integrated with introductory work on process skills and laboratory safety rules as a unit lasting from four to six weeks.

Contexts

Investigations in each unit were framed in industrial and commercial contexts judged likely to appeal to pupils of this age, therefore, tasting and investigating *fizzy drinks* and making *bread*. Our previous experience with context-based approaches in science education, for example, Salters' Science (Campbell et al., 1990), and an analysis of research on the use of these contexts (Bennett et al., 2003) indicated that these types of contexts are motivating and have a positive impact on pupils' attitudes to science.

Letters were used to set contexts for practical investigations carried out by pupils. At the start of work in Y6 and again in Y7 the teacher provided or read out a letter from a (fictitious) company declaring a problem and inviting pupils to carry out investigations to solve it. For example in the Y6 part of the Bread unit pupils were invited by a bakery to investigate whether or not a proving oven would be needed to 'prove' (raise) bread dough. In the Y7 part of this unit, a second letter from the bakery invited pupils to extend their investigations to discover the most suitable range of temperatures and minimum amounts of time that dough would need in the oven. These letters are provided as Text Box 6.1.

Continuity

Teaching and learning in Y6 and Y7 was carefully designed to promote continuity in approach. For example:

- Lessons were planned around a three-part structure – starter activity, main activity, and concluding (plenary) phase – and were presented in common formats.

- Common teaching strategies were used in each phase. These included; the use of posters to help pupils plan investigations (see STAY PDU on the AZSTT website), concept cartoons to stimulate discussion of key ideas (see Keogh and Naylor, 1999) and the letters referred to above.
- Common frameworks were provided for pupils to report findings of investigations and select and use appropriate graphing strategies.
- Emphasis was placed in lesson plans and teacher guidance notes on questioning and learning actions to guide pupils towards considering the status (for example, reliability) of the evidence they obtained from investigations. The aim here was to promote teaching of the *considering and evaluating evidence* strand of Sc1.

Text Box 6.1

Letters used to set contexts for investigations in Y6 and Y7 in the Bread bridging unit

The letter received by Y6 pupils

Lakeside

First for Bread Products

**Lakeside Superstores
Bakery Department
Lakeside Business Park
Laketown**

Dear Primary School Research Team,

We are writing to you in the hope that you can help our Bakery Department.

In the past we have always had our bread dough delivered. To reduce costs, our head office now wants us to mix the dough ourselves.

Could we prove our bread dough at room temperature in an area at the back of the store or do we need a proving oven to be installed?

Please write back to us to tell us what you find out and to advise us on the best action to take.

Yours truly,
Lucy Brown

Lucy Brown
Bakery Manager

The letter received by Y7 pupils

Lakeside

First for Bread Products

Lakeside Superstores
Bakery Department
Lakeside Business Park
Laketown

Dear Secondary School Research Team,

Thank you for the reports from your primary school, which we received in July.

We were particularly interested to read your conclusions about the need to prove our dough above room temperature. As a result, we have contacted an oven manufacturer to design a proving oven.

They now need to know a suitable range of temperatures in order to make the oven. Due to the success of your previous investigation, we would like you to investigate this further.

We would also be interested to know something about the minimum time that the oven would need to be on for so that we are not wasting money.

We look forward to receiving your report.

Yours truly,
Lucy Brown

Lucy Brown
Bakery Manager

Progression

In previous chapters I highlighted the importance of progression in science learning particularly across the primary–secondary transfer. In Chapter 1, I established that school science teaching relies on progression in concepts and procedures and that the two interact. Before developing the STAY bridging units the team looked at what was already available. One commonly used piece of work, 'Bubbles' (Cheshire County Council, n.d.) had the right type of context at each key stage but we could not see how procedural or conceptual knowledge and understanding progressed across transfer. Rather it seemed as if the context was used as a vehicle to develop disparate and disconnected practical work, with little attempt to rationalize conceptual development or to progress it. We decided, therefore, to map carefully the progression within each of the STAY units. The lesson overviews/maps for the Bread unit are provided as an example of this mapping (Text Boxes 6.2 and 6.3). These overviews also show which process skills are the focus of lessons and what activities can be used as extension or enhancement.

Progression in conceptual understanding

In the Bread unit in Y6 the emphasis is on understanding that yeast is an active ingredient making bread dough rise through production of a gas. Through investigation pupils learn that this activity is sensitive to temperature and hence that warm conditions are best for raising (proving) bread dough. In Y7 pupils learn that yeast is a micro-organism, producing carbon dioxide gas as a product of its respiration and that activity is limited by extremes of temperature.

In the Fizzy Drinks unit in Y6 pupils realize that 'fizziness' of a drink is due to the amount of gas it holds (in solution) and that at cold temperatures this is greater. As the drink warms more gas is released and so it goes flat. In Y7, pupils consider what effect the colour of a can has on the warming of drink that it contains. The conceptual area shifts to one connected with heat transfer, absorption of radiated heat and subsequent conduction to the drink contained in different coloured cans. In both Y6 and Y7 pupils use concept cartoons to help them think about what might happen to the gas in a drink when the can is opened. In Y6 the cartoon prompts thinking about the source of gas bubbles when a can is opened. In Y7 the cartoon prompts thinking about what will happen to the mass of a drink when gas escapes from it. These concept cartoons are provided in Text Box 6.4.

Progression in procedural understanding

The practical work in each unit was designed to progress from Y6 to Y7 in terms of procedural demand. The demand of open-ended investigative work is often set by the nature of the variables investigated. This is easiest to see in the variable changed by the investigator – the independent variable. It is assumed that manipulation of a categoric variable (type of floor covering, type of drink) is easier than manipulation of a continuous one (time, temperature, volume, force, and so on). In the Bread unit procedural progression was straightforward. In Y6 lessons pupils chose a place (cold, warm, hot and therefore a categoric variable) to store lumps of dough and measured increase in their size. In Y7, pupils were introduced to the concept of an experimental model – a convenient and controllable test-tube version of reality. They investigated the effect of a range of temperatures (and so a continuous variable) on the quantity (volume or numbers of bubbles of gas) escaping from a tube containing a mixture of yeast, sugar and water.

In Fizzy Drinks, Y6 pupils were invited to explore why fizzy drinks taste better when they are cold. Pupils investigated the rate or quantity of gas

Text Box 6.2

Overview/map of Y6 lessons taught in the Bread unit

Extension	Core lessons	Process skills
Bakery visit or visiting speaker	**Lesson 1** Children learn how bread is made, including the ingredients and the process	Observation Questioning Sequencing Using secondary sources
	Lesson 2 Children see that yeast produces a gas and learn that this shows yeast is active Children explore conditions in which yeast is/is not active	Observing Interpreting
Different groups could pursue different methods	**Lesson 3** Introductory activity on ingredients for bread-making Investigation planning poster encourages class to think about variables affecting rising of bread dough Letter from supermarket bakery to set the specific question to investigate – *How does temp. affect the rise of dough?* Groups plan investigations	Data interpretation Identifying variables Planning investigations
Observation of dough with a magnifying glass	**Lesson 4** Investigations planned in lesson 3 carried out and results recorded	Observation Measurement Collecting and recording data

(Continued)

(Continued)

	Lesson 5	
ICT used to process data and produce graphs	Results from lesson 4 are collated and discussed. Types of graphs are decided on and constructed The class look for patterns in results and suggest optimum conditions for proving dough	Select and draw graphs Seek patterns Explain results
	Lesson 6	
Bake and taste some bread and evaluate the recipe	The class draft a report to send back to the supermarket bakery	Handling data Communicating findings Self assessment

---

Text Box 6.3

Overview/map of Y7 lessons taught in the Bread unit

Extension	**Core lessons**	**Process skills**
	Lesson 1	
Demonstrate variety of breads Different types of bread and recipes explored Tasting session	Recap from Y6 on how bread/dough is made Planning poster used to identify variables that affect rising of bread dough New letter from supermarket bakery introduced and *specific question* for investigation identified. Class plan a method to measure activity of a runny dough mixture at different temperatures	Interpreting data Considering evidence Planning investigations Identifying a suitable range of values to test

(Continued)

	Lesson 2	
Other variables, e.g. yeast type, flour type, amount of sugar, could be investigated ICT: Use of light sensor – see Figure 6.1 on page 90	Class carry out investigations planned in lesson 2 and collect data. They look for patterns and unusual results and calculate means for each temperature tested	Selecting and using equipment Measuring and recording Pattern-seeking Reliability of results
	Lesson 3	
ICT could be used to process data and produce graphs	Results from lesson 2 are collated and graphed. Children are taught about 'error bars' to create a statement about reliability Children are introduced to the idea of 'error bars' on graphs and they draw these and use them to talk about the reliability/accuracy of their results	Graphing Reliability of results
	Lesson 4	
The class could prepare a more, 'in-depth' poster display or prepare to give a research report in an assembly	Children introduced to the concept of yeast as a micro-organism producing CO_2 from respiration (fermentation) Children compare their findings with Y6 outcomes and compose a reply to the supermarket bakery	Graphing Pattern-seeking Considering evidence Reliability of results Self-assessment and target-setting

evolved at different temperatures. In Y7, pupils had to find out why some colours of cans might lead to drinks having 'less fizz'. Because the investigated variable at Y7 was categoric (colour of can) rather than continuous (temperature) as it had been at Y6, we advised secondary teachers in published guidance and in training to ensure that their Y7 pupils investigated *heating rates* for different colours of cans rather than temperature differences for just one colour. This was done to allow for *sufficient progression in*

task demand, in terms of the variables investigated in Y6 and Y7, and so that pupils could develop their abilities to state relationships and comment on reliability of experimental findings. Later in this chapter, results of evaluation are used to see if this happened in practice.

Planned discontinuity

Some writers on primary–secondary transfer caution on the use of work that might be seen by pupils after transfer as simplistic, babyish or too

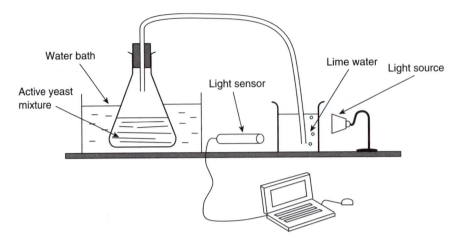

Figure 6.1 Measurement of carbon dioxide evolved from reacting yeast mixture, using a light sensor

rooted in primary experience. For them the move from primary school is an important marker of growing up, and so a certain amount of *discontinuity* of experience is natural and what pupils look forward to and thrive on (Derricott, 1985; Stringer, 2003). This appears to represent a block to bridging but perhaps the trick is to provide what Gorwood (1994) has called a degree of *planned discontinuity*. For example we had a good idea that pupils expect to use more sophisticated equipment when they arrive in secondary school (Braund and Driver, 2005a; Jarman, 1993). The investigations in Y7 were, therefore, designed to allow pupils to use a wider range of different apparatus than is commonly available in primary schools. So we planned for the *discontinuity* of experience with equipment and in laboratories but coupled this with the right amount of *continuity* and progression that we hoped would result in sufficiently challenging new work. In the case of Fizzy Drinks there were opportunities to use ICT, rarely available in the primary school, to enhance measurement. For example in the experimental set-up shown in Figure 6.1, carbon dioxide gas evolved from the reacting yeast mixture is bubbled through lime water (calcium hydroxide) and a light sensor used to measure the optical density as the solution turns 'milky' (with progressive formation of calcium carbonate).

Criticisms of bridging work

Before I turn to evaluation of the STAY bridging units, how pupils and teachers reacted to them, I want to consider a number of criticisms of bridging work. I will then use the findings of evaluation to respond to some of these. Criticisms arise mainly from work by Maurice Galton and his teams (Galton et al., 2003b; 2003c). Though derived from studies of pupils' and teachers' views during the teaching of a mathematics bridging unit, Galton has applied his critique to the use of bridging work in science (Galton, 2002). His main concerns can be summarized as follows:

1 The breakdown of what has been known in the UK as school 'pyramids', where well defined groups of primary schools transfer pupils to just one secondary school, means that not all pupils entering secondary school science classes will have covered the primary part of the bridging unit.
2 Primary teachers and their pupils are not very enthusiastic about the use of these materials after the stresses of national tests carried out in the last term of primary school and the revision period that preceded them.
3 Primary teachers may be unwilling or lack time to mark work at the depth that would be helpful in allowing secondary teachers to develop and progress the topic.
4 Some pupils claim that they rarely see the work that has been transferred or that primary work is only referred to at a superficial level and then the secondary teacher returns to 'business as usual'.
5 Pupils entering secondary school expect and look forward to doing new things. They want to leave their primary experience behind.

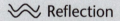 Reflection

Considering your own situation, to what extent is each of Galton's criticisms a block to using bridging work in science? How might any blocks be overcome?

Evaluating impact

A common criticism of projects on transfers and transitions is that few of them have been evaluated in any depth even though substantial sums of money have been spent on them (Galton et al., 1999; Hall et al., 2001; Ofsted, 2002b; Peacock, 1999). We decided to go for a multi-method, naturalistic research design to seek information about bridging work as carried out in some schools and by some teachers in order to provide feedback to these schools and wider audiences (Braund, 2007). Data were collected from pupils and teachers from several different schools that used bridging work, using questionnaires, telephone interviews, group interviews and group discussions. In addition, a more limited study, using tests and retests of pupils' performance on selected items from national tests at Key Stage 2, was carried out in two high schools; one that had been involved in bridging work and one that had not. This part of the evaluation was to determine the impact of science bridging work on pupils' procedural understanding, especially about *considering and evaluating evidence* – one of the key aims of STAY teaching.

Pupils' reactions to bridging work

Over a two-year period, 60 pupils were interviewed in focus groups follow-ing completion of the Fizzy Drinks bridging lessons in Y6 and Y7. This took place in 30 primary schools and in six secondary high schools in two dif-ferent LAs. In the second year of the study it was possible to follow and interview the same pupils from Y6 into Y7. After completing bridging work in Y6, pupils were asked what they felt about carrying on with this work in Y7. After completing the bridging unit in Y7, pupils were again asked to express their feelings about bridging work and to reflect on how useful it had been to them at the start of their secondary school science course.

There was an overwhelmingly positive reaction to bridging work. Over 88 per cent of responses in both age groups were positive. This level was much higher than that reported for a similar bridging project in England (30 per cent) (Davies and McMahon, 2004). The strongest themes evident in both Y6 and Y7 were:

- that bridging work gives a sense of comfort and familiarity at the start of the secondary course
- that bridging work improves confidence in Y7 as a result of experience of practical technique or previous knowledge gained in the work done at primary school
- that the work was not merely a repetition in Y7 of primary experience but was complementary and covered new ground.

A sense of familiarity, for some pupils, included specific reference to the com-fort that recognition of teaching style or approach might bring:

> I thought it was useful because you are doing something you are familiar with even though there were two teachers. It made the Y7 teacher like the Y6 teacher and it helped me. They were using similar words. (Megan, Y7)

Having already established knowledge about the topic and procedures of practical work provided reassurance for many entering Y7:

> I think it's OK learning because if you like do the acids and alkalis (a new topic in secondary school) you wouldn't really learn that in primary school. You'd think 'oh no I'm not good at this', but the cola – you actually know something about it so you can talk to your teacher a bit more about it when you have finished it ... (Katy, Y7)

One of Galton's most prominent critiques of bridging work (number 5 in the list above) is that pupils might see Y7 work as mere repetition of topics and procedures already covered and that this runs against what they are looking forward to in secondary science (Galton, 2002). Although com-ments about repetition were not the most frequent, pupils in both years did make specific and positive references to it, for example:

I feel that it's better doing it more than once because you will find out different stuff. Not the same stuff you found out this time ... different stuff, what the coke was made from or something. (Briony, Y6)

In Davies and McMahon's study 25 per cent of Y7 pupils thought of work as mere repetition of Y6. In the STAY project the equivalent figure was much lower, at only 8 per cent.

The use of planning posters, included to ensure continuity, seemed to have struck a chord with the pupils at both ages and was mentioned specifically by about half of the pupils interviewed at each age (12 pupils in Y6 and 16 pupils in Y7).

We had a sheet like, on a big special board (a large laminated planning poster). ... we filled that in as a class and he (the teacher) let us blitz ideas down onto the board and then he showed us where we were going off track and where we were on track and we eventually altogether made it. (Alastair, Y7)

Examples of planning posters and how they can be used in teaching of bridging lessons can be viewed or downloaded from the STAY project professional development unit (PDU) which is available on the AZSTT website (see after References).

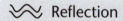 Reflection

What other teaching techniques (like planning posters) could be used either side of transfer to promote continuity in science learning?

Teachers' reactions to bridging work

Teachers in 21 of the 49 primary schools teaching Fizzy Drinks were interviewed by telephone. Seventeen of these teachers were interviewed one year later having taught the second unit, Bread. Co-ordinators for Key Stage 3 science in secondary schools that taught Fizzy Drinks collected views from teachers in their schools and these views were discussed at a special meeting held by the LA.

We found that primary teachers were very positive about bridging work in science. Contrary to Galton's claim that primary teachers are largely unenthusiastic about teaching bridging work (number 2 in the list above), there were no negative comments concerning the validity or usefulness of bridging work. Responses showed general acceptance of the bridging work as a sound foundation and preparation for further study.

It's familiarity that's the key ... knowing they (pupils) will be continuing work on Fizzy Drinks and that pupils from other schools would be doing that too. It allows them to look forward and to see a point to their activities.

From their (pupils') point of view it has a ring of continuity and is like secondary. It's good to break down barriers between the two phases.

For some teachers (5/21 teaching Fizzy Drinks and 8/17 teaching Bread), however, this acceptance was qualified by concerns that work might not be continued in, or sufficiently valued by, secondary schools.

> There's lots of in-depth stuff in this work and that will be good for secondary. I think it's great from the primary end but I just hope they (teachers) pick it up at the secondary school. I have my doubts though.

> It all depends on what happens next in the secondary school. They (teachers) might just say – well you've measured the rise of dough but now we are going to investigate bread again – but properly this time. There is a danger that the high schools might miss what lessons are trying to achieve.

This seems to reiterate fears expressed in point four of Galton's critique about the quality of response to work transferred. There were also a number of concerns about the use of the assessment scheme, but these are addressed in detail in Chapter 8.

We asked primary teachers to identify anything from the teaching of bridging work that might influence future teaching of science. One specific strategy, the use of planning posters seemed, as was the case for pupils, to have been popular with a number of teachers (11/21 and 12/17).

> Post-it planners – fantastic – I used one big poster with the whole class and will definitely be using this again. It's a brilliant technique and it's something that we are considering for science lessons across Key Stage 2.

Some teachers claimed that teaching bridging work had prompted them to rethink the focus and balance of their teaching.

> I want to do more investigations and spend more time on considering evidence, particularly 'trusting results'. It (teaching Fizzy Drinks) made me realize that investigations aren't just about 'fair testing' or 'whole investigations'.

Most Key Stage 3 co-ordinators from secondary schools that taught Fizzy Drinks felt the bridging work had been of value and said their pupils enjoyed carrying it out. Their comments were at times rather less enthusiastic and guarded than those of their primary colleagues. The following is an example:

> Lots of them (pupils) had 'forgotten' what they'd done, and many hadn't done it (bridging work) in year 6. Not sure how it will help transfer – not convinced there has even been a problem. Some children were bored because they felt it was repetitive.

Co-ordinators in two schools thought their pupils were bored by the work. Interestingly, this was not corroborated by comments made by pupils in these schools when groups of pupils were interviewed. As with the Y6 teachers, Key Stage 3 co-ordinators were asked to say if teachers in their schools thought that the practical skills of their pupils had improved as a result of carrying out work on Fizzy Drinks. Responses to this item were much more varied than for Y6 teachers. Four of the nine schools felt that practical skills had advanced no more than would have been expected through carrying out work usually done at this stage in Y7. As for Y6 teachers, comments from secondary schools about the use of the assessment scheme are dealt with separately in Chapter 8.

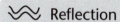 Reflection

As a head of science in a secondary school, what steps would you take to 'pave the way' for using bridging units in science?

The impact of bridging on pupils' procedural understanding

We selected questions relating to three areas of procedural understanding from national test papers in science taken by pupils at the end of Key Stage 2:

Type 1 questions assessed pupils' abilities to identify and/or extract data presented as tables and graphs.

Type 2 questions assessed pupils' abilities in planning investigations, for example, by asking them to comment on the question addressed by an investigation or to identify and/or select independent, dependent or controlled variables for an investigation.

Type 3 questions assessed pupils' abilities to identify patterns and/or relationships in data or to comment on the validity of conclusions made.

Pupils' scores for these questions were obtained from the test papers taken at the end of Key Stage 2 and we retested them using these same questions after ten weeks in their new secondary schools. Two groups of pupils were identified: pupils who had been taught the Fizzy Drinks unit (the experimental group) and pupils that had not (the control group). All other teaching between the two groups was as similar as possible and the groups were matched in terms of the social background and performance data of their schools (Braund, 2007: 918–20). The results of the study are shown in Table 6.1.

Effect sizes were calculated for each group by taking the difference between mean scores at each age, divided by the standard deviation of the scores of the control group. Effect sizes are increasingly used in education research to assess the likely impact of an intervention (Cohen, 1969; Glass et al., 1981). Its advocates argue that it communicates more clearly than a statistical significance

Table 6.1 Change in pupils' performance on questions on scientific enquiry selected from Key Stage 2 national tests

	Experimental group		Control group		Effect	
	Mean change of score	Standard deviation	Mean change of score	Standard deviation	Difference in mean change of score *Experimental – Control*	Effect size
Whole test (max=33)	−1.4	4.5	−2.2	4.2	0.8	0.19
Type 1 (max=5)	−0.2	0.9	−0.2	1.0	0.0	0.0
Type 2 (max=8)	1.3	1.7	0.8	1.7	0.5	0.29
Type 3 (max=20)	−1.9	3.2	−1.5	3.1	−0.4	−0.13

level how well an intervention works. For a fuller discussion of the use of effect sizes in educational research, see Coe (2002).

The overall pattern shown in the comparison of pupils' performance shown in Table 6.1 was one of regression. This was to be expected, given results of studies reported previously, in Chapter 2. The reduction in the mean mark for pupils in the experimental group in this study was, however, less than that for the pupils in the control group. While the effect size was small (0.19) the intervention (bridging) can be said to have had a modest impact if we compare it with effect sizes quoted for a range of other studies with similar age groups in other areas of education, such as reading, spelling and so on (Lipsey and Wilson, 1993). It is worth noting that the amounts of regression for the experimental group in this study was less than that found by Nicholls and Gardner (1999).

Analysis of pupils' performance by each of the three question types showed that there was a different pattern of performance for each type. In type 2 questions, concerned with planning scientific investigations, the pattern was one of modest progression rather than regression. While both groups of pupils progressed, there was a small but marked difference in favour of pupils in the experimental group (effect size, 0.29). This suggests that it was relative progression in the process skills of planning and identification of variables that contributed most of the difference in the retest results between the two groups of pupils. Since the ability to identify and comment on relationships, patterns and evidence supporting conclusions (as represented by type three questions) was a major part of the teaching of bridging lessons this was rather worrying. Results seem to show that these abilities were not advanced as much as the planning of investigations. It could be that schools ignored advice about procedural progression in Fizzy Drinks. If pupils in Y7 did no more than measure the heat rise for one or more colours of cans instead of charting the temperature rise over time (for one or more colour of can), then the intended progression from investigating a categoric variable to a continuous one did not happen. There was support for this conclusion when pupils were interviewed. Fewer pupils in Y7 compared with Y6 could make statements that related patterns of experimental outcomes to what had been changed and measured (Braund and Hames, 2005). It seems that care is needed in dissemination and training before teachers get to use these units, so that they more clearly appreciate the progression lines on which teaching is based.

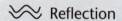 Reflection

Look at two examples of scientific investigations used in similar context areas in Y6 and Y7. Is the progression in procedural demand (the nature of variables investigated or changed) sufficient to provide the right degree of challenge and progression? If not how would you change the investigations to improve progression and challenge?

The true worth of bridging in science

Evaluation shows that there are key benefits for teachers and pupils in primary schools from using science bridging work, if it is designed carefully and taught well. The intentions for bridging in science seem to have borne fruit. Where they did not, we felt this was most likely to have been when schools were half-hearted about doing it, thought the work was too demanding and time-consuming or that their pupils would benefit more from doing something else. Schools (both primary and secondary) gained most when the key messages about science teaching embedded in the units – concentrating on reliability of findings, using common and recognizable teaching strategies and language, and recognizing procedural progression – were taken on board, rather than just teaching the lessons as something else for pupils to do. Best practice in secondary schools seems to have much to do with how well bridging work is integrated with other efforts to improve transfer in science, such as co-observation of each other's teaching, meetings to compare standards of work, induction visits, and so on. A bridging unit is just part of a complex of strategies that will hopefully have an impact on pupils and help raise standards in Key Stage 3. At least bridging work is something that is now available, has been well researched and can be used to help achieve this aim.

Chapter summary

Bridging units in science require careful planning so that the correct directions and amounts of progression in procedural and conceptual demand are provided. Discontinuities should also be planned so that pupils appreciate and enjoy the experience of doing science in new surroundings. In contrast to criticisms of bridging work in science and other studies, evaluations show that pupils do enjoy bridging work at both sides of transfer, although secondary teachers can be more sceptical than their primary counterparts. Best practice in bridging is seen when the key messages about continuity and progression in teaching and learning are grasped, and when bridging is used alongside other strategies to improve primary–secondary transfer in science.

Suggested actions

- At meetings, primary and secondary teachers share approaches that help pupils see consistency in structures that help them apply and develop process skills. Planning posters and investigation/graphing writing frames are particularly helpful.
- Use letters and emails to set contexts for investigative work.
- Make sure that co-planned work has sufficient progression in procedural demand (for example, types and nature of variables investigated) either side of transfer and that both sets of teachers using materials understand and stick to progression lines.
- Talk to pupils about what they have done in primary school and, if using bridging units, make sure that the work done in Y6 is recapped in the first few lessons.

7

Beyond Bridging

Chapter overview

Scientific Enquiry Progression Tasks (SEPTs) provide flexible approaches to teaching for progression and continuity across transfer. Progression steps in one example, Mouldy Old Dough, are explored in detail. Teachers' reactions to using SEPTs and insights gained through teaching them are reviewed.

In the previous chapter I made the case for bridging work in science as a way of providing the right amount of continuity (and planned discontinuity) while ensuring sufficient progression – without repetition of work. These are things that, with careful design and understanding of key principles, can be achieved. On this basis I think that bridging in science is successful and valued by teachers and pupils. Using bridging units, however, requires a commitment both in terms of teaching time and willingness for schools to participate both sides of transfer. One of Galton's criticisms of bridging work, that I included in the previous chapter, is that clusters of primary schools feeding just one secondary school (or pyramids as they have been called) have broken down and so the necessary degree of co-operation and co-ordination may no longer exist (Galton, 2002). This is largely attributed to the emergence of the education marketplace in England where parents are now able to apply for places at any one of a number of competing secondary schools rather than admissions being geographically allocated by LAs. The result is that it is no longer possible to guarantee that all pupils in a Y6 class in primary school X will go to secondary school Y. When teaching a bridging unit in science this could mean that the Y7 teacher might have a class in which some pupils have done the primary part of the bridging unit but many others have not. This was of real concern in one school in York when teaching the Fizzy Drinks unit. The school in question is a Catholic denominational (voluntarily aided) high school drawing pupils from 30 different primary schools spread across several hundred square kilometres. In this case, Y7 teachers grouped pupils who had done the Y6 lessons with those who had not. Teachers in this school told me that, while not as good as all or most pupils completing both sets of lessons, this arrangement worked quite well. They claimed that having to remember and explain accurately what had been done before to others provided social cohesion and helped pupils settle into their new environment. Teachers told us that 40 per cent having done the Y6 part was a minimum requirement for this to work – anything less would be problematic. Teams developing other bridging work in science concur that this minimum limit for participation is about right (Davies and McMahon, 2004).

As I reported in the previous chapter, teachers using STAY bridging units in primary schools were overwhelmingly supportive of the approach. There were, however, one or two Y6 teachers with wider responsibility for the whole curriculum of their schools who were more critical. The comments of two such teachers are revealing and worth considering in some detail:

> I'm a bit mixed. I mean you say to us – 'How about another transfer unit?' It's almost like each subject wants the best out of the children – but we have to do all 3 (in English, mathematics and science). It's hard going. I mean when secondary teachers have done their exams – it's like what do they have to do? We finish ours (national tests) and then we've got all this stuff (bridging work) to do for the secondary school. (P1: a Y6 teacher who was also an assistant head teacher in charge of the curriculum)

> OK, but we had too much to do and we had a big sex education unit to do and this really suffered. We think it's important to do it (the sex education unit) well. Design and Technology suffered as a result and doing all this bridging stuff ... and this (the sex education unit) is normally a great unit of work for us and them (the pupils). (P2: a Y6 teacher who was also a co-ordinator for science and technology)

Although these were relatively lone voices among teachers we interviewed, their comments deserve to be taken seriously. Striking a balance between teaching bridging work and providing other experiences that are equally valid and of interest to pupils at this stage in their schooling is clearly seen by these teachers as being important. In a survey of head teachers conducted by advisory staff in the City of York following the second year of bridging, comments showed that units (in mathematics, English and science) were clearly valued, but that there were concerns about the time commitment required to teach all three of them effectively.

A more flexible approach

It was apparent from our work that, while teachers valued and might continue using bridging units, they also wanted to have at their disposal more flexible approaches that do not require specified teaching blocks either side of transfer. To explore how this might be done, a project funded by the AZSTT, was set up called the North Yorkshire AstraZeneca Science Pedagogy and Progression (NYASPP) Project. Before writing any materials, the NYASPP team took on board the key findings of the STAY project and other research, namely that:

- Secondary pupils in Y7 classes value and feel comfortable and confident with familiar teaching approaches met before in Y6 (such as concept cartoons and the use of investigation planning posters).
- Pupils in Y7 classes often repeat practical work done before in primary school without any additional challenge. They find this boring and demotivating.
- Teachers in both phases value a context-based approach to science but sometimes lack the means to make this happen. There is evidence that context-based approaches are valued by pupils and help maintain positive attitudes.
- Teachers value improved understanding of the ways in which each other work including how the language of teaching and learning can be made more contiguous either side of transfer.
- There has been a significant and serious reduction in the amount of practical work done in Y6 classes. This has widened the gap between Y6 and Y7 teaching and has encouraged pupils and teachers to regard the use and application of what should be commonly used science skills as discontinuous. This encourages teachers to use a 'fresh start' approach and leads pupils to believe that what they did before is not valued.
- Teachers in both phases are looking for ways to link good quality opportunities for a range of types of scientific enquiry to their current schemes of work.

As a prelude to writing the materials, the NYASPP team used the activity described in Chapter 2 (see Text Box 2.1) to help pairs of primary and secondary teachers identify practical work that might be used both sides of transfer. In doing this we did not restrict the activity to just experiences in Y6 and Y7, but opened this out to practical work that might be used in any year in the upper part of the primary school (Years 4–6, age 9–11) and in all years of Key Stage 3 (Years 7–9, age 11–14). This led to the identification of a number topics where progression steps could be set out in more detail. A key question emerged: 'If this is what is most appropriately taught and experienced at Key Stage 2, how would the same topic and similar practical work be taught at Key Stage 3 so that tasks are challenging enough and not merely seen as repetition by pupils?' Thus the idea was to show primary and secondary teachers how procedures and knowledge gained by primary pupils can be recognized, built on and developed.

Scientific Enquiry Progression Tasks

The NYASPP team established the concept of a *Scientific Enquiry Progression Task* or SEPT. Four such tasks were produced on the basis that they could be shared with teachers who could then go on to replicate the process in their own schools by devising tasks in whatever topic they might wish to develop and progress each side of transfer. The process still requires a degree of co-operation and agreement between primary and secondary teachers but has the advantage that tasks are not so time consuming and are likely to dovetail more easily with existing teaching. The model of school science based on dual, integrated progression of procedural and conceptual knowledge and understanding, described in Chapter 1, persuaded us that progression lines in both areas should be made highly visible in each SEPT. Table 7.1 outlines the four SEPTs produced by the NYASPP team and the procedural and conceptual progression lines in each of them.

In the next section one SEPT is explored in some detail to show more clearly how they were designed.

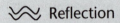

Reflection

Select a topic taught both sides of transfer and devise steps like those in Table 7.1 to show how process skills and concepts would be progressed.

Mouldy Old Dough

Before organizing pairs comprising primary and secondary teachers as NYASPP writing teams for each SEPT, we agreed a common framework for writing the materials.

An overview	This summarizes what pupils are asked to do in each key stage.
Position in teaching	This suggests how SEPTs might fit with other teaching.
References	These show how the work relates to the National Curriculum for science and to the QCA schemes of work for KS2 and KS3 (DfEE/QCA, 2000a; 2000b).
Expected progression from KS2 to KS3	This sets out how tasks progress pupils' process skills of scientific enquiry (procedural understanding) and their knowledge and understanding of science ideas (conceptual understanding).
Links forward to KS3	Suggestions as to what teachers might say to pupils in KS2 to help link forward to work they might do in KS3.
Links back to KS2	Suggestions as to what teachers in KS3 might say to pupils to help them recognize achievements from KS2 and make links to work they have done before without pupils seeing work as merely repetition.

Table 7.1 Scientific Enquiry Progression Tasks and examples of progression from KS2 to KS3

	Procedural progression		Conceptual progression	
	KS2	KS3	KS2	KS3
Mouldy Old Dough	Sequence pictures of mould growth allocating percentages to each	Give numerical values to observations of mould growth	Various moulds grow on bread	Mould growth is limited by available resources, e.g. space, food
Finding a solution	Explain dissolving rates drawing on experimental evidence (e.g. of the effects of particle size, temperature and stirring)	Draw on experimental evidence and information from graphs using the concept of saturation (of a solution)	Some solids dissolve more readily than others and solution rates are affected by a number of factors	There is a limit to the quantity of solid that can dissolve in a set volume of liquid
Lighting up	Predict the effect of varying types and lengths of wire on the brightness of bulbs in a circuit	Predict the effect of varying lengths and thicknesses of wire and measure flow (current) in a circuit using an ammeter	Different materials conduct electricity to different extents	The flow of electricity in a circuit depends on the ease with which it can flow in a conductor (resistance)
Stretchy things	Measure accurately in Newtons (N). Draw graphs using given axes	Draw a line graph and make predictions from it. Extract and explain patterns from graphs	Stretch of elastic depends on the amount of force put on it	There is a limit to the amount of force that can be applied to a spring

An example of how this framework was applied for one of the SEPTs, Mouldy Old Dough, is provided as Text Box 7.1.

One of the most important aspects of SEPTs was how teachers might make explicit links between pupils' experiences at each key stage. This was done to avoid what we called the, 'Please miss/sir we've done all this before' syndrome. By this we meant that some pupils in secondary science classes have a tendency to state something is repetition merely on sight of a piece of equipment or on reading/hearing an experiment title. So, for example, as soon as the secondary teacher brings out a force meter and tells the class that they are to investigate which trainer has the most friction, pupils might automatically assume this is the same as any investigation where they used a force meter to measure friction in primary school. It matters little to pupils that progression steps have been carefully planned by the teacher. For example the teacher in secondary school might now intend that pupils choose the correct range of force meter to measure accurately or that differences in amounts of force to get the trainer moving (to overcome its inertia) compared to when it is being pulled across the surface are now the focus of the work. For many pupils the mere presence of familiar equipment or titles of tasks spark superficial, episodic memories that often result in rejection and disappointment. So we wanted to encourage teachers in both key stages to make explicit links both forwards and backwards, as suggested by Jarman (1997), so that pupils can readily appreciate what they have done before and will do in the future, and recognize this as progression rather than repetition. For example in the SEPT called Mouldy Old Dough, after completion of tasks in the primary school, the Key Stage 2 teacher was encouraged to:

> Discuss with children that there are many ways to present results. In KS2 they have used one method to present mould growth as a percentage and have chosen the right graph to show data. In secondary school they will learn that different microbes such as mould can be isolated and studied to see how each one grows. (Braund et al., 2004: 8)

Before the Key Stage 3 teacher prepares work on a related topic, they should be encouraged to recognize and value primary school experience and show clearly how this 'fits' with what pupils will do now. For example we advised Key Stage 3 teachers that they might:

> Remind pupils that in their primary schools they were able to match mould growth with percentages and began to make decisions about the most appropriate graphs to present their data. Tell them that now they are in secondary school they will build on these skills to explore how microbes like mould can be independently grown on agar plates so that the rate of their growth can be studied and measured more accurately. (Braund et al., 2004: 8)

Text Box 7.1

An example of a Scientific Enquiry Progression Task, Mouldy Old Dough

Overview

Pupils translate observed data from pictures of mould on bread into numerical forms. In Key Stage 2 they do this by matching percentage cards with pictures showing mouldy bread. In Key Stage 3 they work out a numerical value for cover of a specific mould (*Penecillium*) growing on an agar plate. In both key stages pupils select appropriate graphs to show pattern of mould growth over time. Additionally, in Key Stage 3, pupils construct line graphs and respond to questions about growth rate.

Key Stage 2	Key Stage 3
The lesson could be taught mid-way through a unit of work (6B: Micro-organisms). Activities could be used as part of a revision programme or as stand-alone, skills-related activities with some prior input on microbes.	The lesson could be taught early in a unit of work (e.g. 8C: Microbes and disease). Activities could be used to address limiting factors to population growth (8D: Ecological relationships).
NC KS2 PoS: Sc2 5f; Micro-organisms. Sc1, 2i,j; Communicating findings and considering evidence. **QCA unit**: 6B: Micro-organisms.	**NC KS3 PoS**: Sc2 5d; Population sizes and resources. Sc1, 2i-n; Communicating findings, considering evidence including anomalies. **QCA units**: 8C: Microbes and disease; 8D: Ecological relationships.
Expected progression in process skills: At KS2 most children would be expected to: • sequence pictures of mould growth and allocate percentage coverage to each • understand that some methods of presenting data are more suitable than others • match pattern statements with shapes of line graphs.	**Expected progression in process skills**: At KS3 most children would be expected to: • convert pictorial evidence into numerical data • draw a line graph with suitable scale, axes and title • use a line graph to predict growth rates. Identify trends and explain an anomalous result.

(Continued)

(Continued)

Expected progression in science ideas: At KS2 most children would be expected to:	Expected progression in science ideas: At KS3 most children would be expected to:
• know that different moulds grow on bread over a period of time.	• realize that mould growth rate varies over time and that it is limited by resources.

In the Mouldy Old Dough SEPT the key learning activity ensuring progression, as outlined in Table 7.1, involved pupils at each key stage translating observations of mould growth on bread into quantitative data. As in the bridging units, discussed in the previous chapter, associated concepts were explored at each key stage using concept cartoons, thereby helping ensure continuity of teaching. These are provided in Text Box 7.2.

The Key Stage 2 'cartoon' dealt with pupils' conceptions of the source of mould on sandwiches in a lunch box found in a child's bedroom. At Key Stage 3 the context shifted to one where one mould species growing on bread is isolated and grown on Petri dishes. The cartoon now requires pupils to think about the rate at which the mould will grow.

The main learning activity at Key Stage 2 involves pupils sequencing sets of randomly assorted time-lapse images of mould growth and deciding how amount of growth might be given numerical values, for example, as a percentage of the bread covered by mould. These time-lapse images are provided as part of Text Box 7.3. Pupils were shown various ways in which the results could be presented as graphs and discussed in groups which graphing method might be most appropriate to use and why.

At Key Stage 3 pupils are shown images of mouldy bread and introduced to the idea that there are several types or species of mould that develop and have covered different amounts of the bread. This leads to the idea that different types of moulds might grow at different rates and that to study the growth of one type involves isolating it and growing it on a special sterile medium (agar in a Petri dish). The main activity at Key Stage 3 requires pupils to come up with ways of measuring the amount of mould that has developed on Petri dishes after certain amounts of time. Of course this can be done using real cultures as long as safety rules have been obeyed (see, for example, CLEAPSS, 2001) but for those teachers who wished to use a paper activity we provided a set of diagrams for this activity, as shown in Text Box 7.4.

Text Box 7.2

Concept cartoon used in the Mouldy Old Dough SEPT at Key Stage 2

Where did the
mould come from?

I think mould was in the
bread to start with.

I think mould came
from the air.

I think mould came from
the plastic of the box.

What do you think?

(Continued)

(Continued)

Concept cartoon used in the Mouldy Old Dough SEPT at Key Stage 3

How quickly does mould grow?

I think the mould will grow the same amount each day.

I think the mould will grow fastest in the first four days.

I think the mould will grow a bit then stop and then grow a lot more.

I think the mould will grow fast at first and then slow down.

What do you think?

Text Box 7.3

Mould on bread cards used for the KS2 activity in the Mouldy Old Dough SEPT

In trials of the SEPT, pupils came up with a number of ways of quantifying mould growth for each time period:

- Approximate cover of mould was given a fractional or percentage value.
- The diameter of the 'colonies' was measured.
- The circumferences of 'colonies' was measured using string.
- The surface area of 'colonies' was approximated using a transparent grid.

Pupils discussed the accuracy of different measures they used and results were presented as graphs. At Key Stage 3 the choice of graph type and axes was left up to pupils though help was given according to individual needs.

Teachers' reactions to using Scientific Enquiry Progression Tasks

The NYASPP project that produced SEPTs was not researched to the same extent as STAY bridging work described in the previous chapter. However, some of the teachers using the materials were interviewed following trials of the learning materials and observations of teaching using SEPTs in the alternative phase to the one in which they normally taught. Responses, especially from secondary teachers, showed significant insights as a result of using SEPTs. For example on the matter of recognizing levels of previous

Text Box 7.4

Mould growth diagrams used for KS3

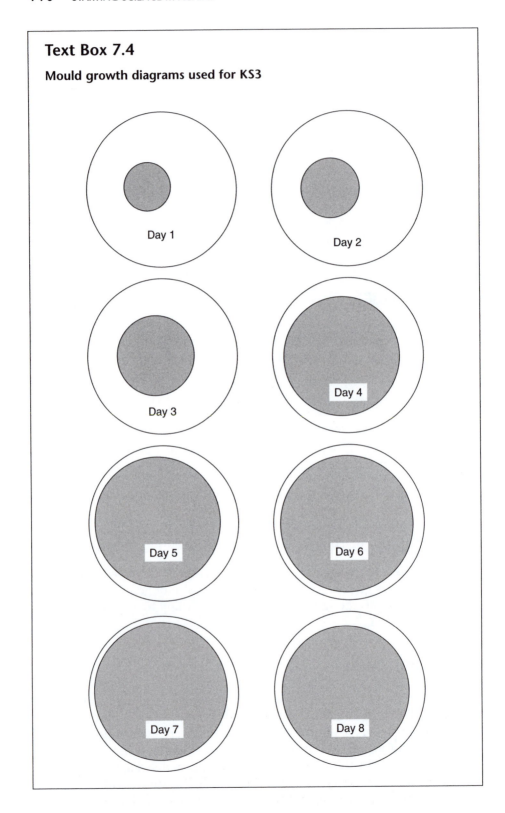

work and knowledge, Bob, an experienced head of science in a secondary school noted:

> Yes, I mean we have been saying this all the time about taking on board what kids know and I realize now that we have got to actually say to kids, 'what do you know' before we start on a topic ... especially there is a lot more now being done on Sc1 and on 'How science works' than I thought because they are getting worried about it ... really seriously worried about what sort of questions might be in SATs.

Bob's response challenges evidence on declining amounts of practical work in the final year of primary school discussed in Chapters 3 and 4. His perception was that a change in the national tests at Key Stage 2, which now include more questions testing procedural knowledge, might have led to more work requiring pupils to consider and evaluate evidence gained from practical work. He clearly believed that the levels pupils were capable of working at had implications for what is taught in his own school.

Another head of science in a secondary school, Sarah, could see from watching teaching in her feeder primary schools, that the way in which some primary schools teach science has much to tell her about pupils' attitudes and the importance of valuing their previous experiences:

> It reminded me of the 'magical' science that captures imaginations at KS1 and KS2 and how we secondary teachers do not always take that knowledge and enthusiasm and go with it. It has refocused my teaching and made me refer back to and project forward to where things are leading to.

Finally, a third secondary teacher, Gill, could see implications beyond just Y7:

> It has been very interesting to collaborate with the primary schools and it's made me think definitely about my teaching of Year 7 ... but also about Y8. I think that obviously there is a knock on effect from Year 7 isn't there? If you are challenging Year 7 as well as you could do. I think you tend to think of Year 7 as the babies but in actual fact they are coming in and know far more and use far more scientific language than you think.

According to Galton et al. (1999; 2003b) Y8 is possibly the most problematic year of the secondary school as that is when attitudes, particularly in science, seem to dip most. Gill's comments here seem to be saying that, 'if we get the challenge and progress right in Year 7 then we have to maintain the same amounts of challenge and progress thereafter'.

Perhaps the most important outcome of using bridging units or the progression tasks described in this chapter is the improved insights they bring on important matters like differences in teaching and learning and maintaining sufficient progression and continuity. Engaging in these sorts of activities forces these issues to be explored at first hand, rather than through discussion, meetings and by scanning policy and curriculum documents. Having to use and engage with these materials, and reflect on using them, opens up new spaces for professional dialogue. The real value, though, probably comes when teaching is also observed or even when teachers co-teach using the materials in each others' classes. How this can be done most effectively and what can be achieved by doing this is the subject of Chapter 9.

Summary

Scientific Enquiry Progression Tasks provide additional and useful insights on progression and continuity across the KS2–KS3 transfer. At the core of SEPTs is the importance of referring back to and valuing what has been done in primary school, thereby reinforcing for pupils that science learning is a continuum. What is learned and practised then becomes the platform for further development of ideas and application and for development of procedures and skills.

Suggested actions

- Ask teachers to look at examples of topics and practical work taught in adjacent key stages. Ask them to devise progression steps using the framework described in this chapter.
- Get teachers to script what the KS2 and KS3 teacher will say to pupils about similar topics and tasks used at each key stage. These can be prefaced with, 'looking forward to ...' and 'using what we have learned before ...'.

8

In the Know: Using Assessment and Recording to Improve Transfer in Science

Chapter overview

Comparing standards either side of transfer remains one of the most impenetrable issues of primary–secondary transfer, especially for science. Some reasons for this are reviewed. Two versions of a system to provide formative assessment information in bridging work and feedback from teachers who used them are discussed. Another transfer record, the pupils' passport, is described. Methods used in liaison meetings to review pupils' use and application of science process skills either side of transfer are featured.

Assessment has traditionally been one of the thorniest problems of KS2/3 transfer and not only in science. Providing assessment information that is meaningful and getting secondary teachers to make use of it when it is, are recurring issues at different transfer ages. Problems are not only products of legislation such as the National Curriculum. For example, in a study of transfer practices at ages 9 and 13 in the Isle of Wight in the early 1980s, it was found that communication between schools about assessment lacked focus and that transfer of pupils' grades did little to help them make progress (Stillman and Maychell, 1984). One might expect that, with all the efforts that have been made on transition and transfer over the past quarter of a century since this survey took place, the situation might now be much improved. However, according to Her Majesty's Chief Inspector of schools, although a general improvement is recognized, transferring and using assessment information remain as significant blots on the transfer landscape. 'Although planning for the transfer from primary to secondary education had improved (since 2004–5) and was satisfactory in a large majority of schools, the transfer of assessment and other data was still unsatisfactory in nearly a quarter of secondary schools' (Ofsted, 2006: para. 249, 59).

A number of reports, based on detailed surveys, have highlighted specific problems:

- KS3 teachers distrust the levels of attainment that pupils have been assessed at in primary schools. In some cases this is because there are different interpretations of national criteria (levels) against which work is judged or beliefs that levels of attainment are artificially 'jacked-up' by revision for tests. These matters were discussed in detail in Chapter 4.
- Despite national and regional arrangements, the amount and quality of assessment information transferred and reaching science departments in secondary schools is inconsistent (Ofsted, 2002b; Peacock, 1999).
- Assessment information transferred to the secondary school is often ignored or is not detailed enough to guide effective lesson planning that takes account of pupils' individual abilities (Lee et al., 1995; Nicholls and Gardner, 1999; Schagen and Kerr, 1999).
- Portfolios or examples of pupils' work are infrequently made available to secondary schools. While this is often common practice in English/literacy it is rare in science, as a study in Worcester LA showed (see Peacock, 1999). Where this does happen (in one-fifth of cases in Worcestershire schools) work is rarely used or referred to by the receiving teachers. Consequently, pupils feel their efforts and achievements in primary science are not valued.

Designing a 'user-friendly' assessment and transfer system

Recognizing these problems, teams at York decided that an assessment and transfer system would be carefully devised and provided for schools using the bridging units described in Chapter 6. Before designing the system itself we devised a MUST list that we think can be applied to assessment systems in general.

Any assessment system MUST be:

Manageable: in the sense that it is rooted in a planning-learning-assessment cycle driven by the needs of learners rather than the unmanageable tick lists and form-filling that have been unfortunate and frequent products of national curriculum assessment practices in the UK (Black and Wiliam, 2005). The system must be relatively unburdensome for teachers to use in terms of its complexity and the time required to use it.

Usable: assessment information has to be of the right quality and level of detail to help teachers develop, challenge and progress pupils' learning.

Systematic: assessment should be located within schemes of work and equitably planned, used and monitored across a term, a school year or even a whole key stage.

Targeted: to ensure that assessment is *manageable, systematic* and *usable*, at the classroom level it must *target* a few concepts or skills or be used for assessing a few individuals.

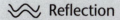

Reflection

Critically evaluate an assessment scheme with which you are familiar using the MUST criteria. How would you adapt or change the scheme to meet these criteria?

With the MUST mnemonic in mind, the York team also wanted to draw on best practice in assessment, particularly seminal work on formative and diagnostic assessment by Black and Wiliam (1998) and Black et al. (2002). According to Black and Wiliam's meta-analysis of research on assessment, when used well, formative assessment produces significant and substantial learning gains, indeed, more so than from many other teaching interventions (Black and Wiliam, 1998). Many of the studies they looked at showed that low-attaining pupils benefit particularly. Research also shows the importance of pupils being actively involved in the process and of assessment being used to inform future learning. Formative comments alone have more impact on pupils' learning than comments accompanied by either marks or grades. A crucial feature of formative assessment is that pupils are given feedback on how to improve their work. Pupil self-assessment is seen as an essential aspect of formative assessment, as it helps pupils understand the main purpose of their learning. This implies that pupils should be given clear and under-standable criteria by which they can judge work they produce. With these principles and findings in mind the York team set about designing the assessment and transfer record shown in Text Box 8.1.

The scheme was designed to be used by pupils and their teachers before and after using bridging work in Y6, and to be continued after transfer and throughout Y7 and beyond if the receiving teacher so desired.

Using the scheme

Instructions provided for Y6 teachers
1 Before you start teaching the bridging unit lessons, use the pupil self-review sheet with your pupils so that they can review their current performance. Advise pupils to complete column one of the record, thinking carefully about how they might be doing against each of the statements. Pupils should then enter a number into each circle, chosen according to the following criteria:

Choosing ① if they think they can do this well in all lessons.
Choosing ② if they think they can do this most of the time.

Text Box 8.1

Transfer record used for STAY project bridging units

Name _____

In Year 6 I investigated …	
Date:	School:
In Year 7 I investigated …	
Date:	School:

	When I carry out scientific enquiries	Y6	Y6	Y7	Y7
Planning	I can decide what to change	O	O	O	O
	I can decide what to measure	O	O	O	O
	I can decide what to keep the same to make it a fair test	O	O	O	O
	I can make a prediction and use science to explain it	O	O	O	O
	I can predict the shape of graph I expect to get	O	O	O	O
Obtaining + Presenting	I can choose useful measurements to make	O	O	O	O
	I can take repeated measurements and work out averages	O	O	O	O
	I can draw my own table for my results	O	O	O	O
	I can draw a bar graph of my results	O	O	O	O
	I can draw a line graph of my results	O	O	O	O
Considering evidence	I can describe the pattern in my results	O	O	O	O
	I can explain my results using some science I know	O	O	O	O
	I can describe how careful and accurate my measurements were	O	O	O	O
	I can explain whether I can trust my results	O	O	O	O

Year 6 Teacher's Comments

Year 7 Teacher's Comments

Choosing ③ if they think they sometimes need help from others to do this.

Choosing ④ if they think they need help with this most of the time.

2   Towards the end of the unit (lesson 5 or 6), repeat the self-review with the class, reminding them of the process described above. Tell pupils to use column two of the record. Allow pupils time to recognize and celebrate progress that they think has been made.

3   Collect individual records and read them.

4   On each pupil's sheet, highlight up to three aspects (in any areas) that you think, as their teacher, each pupil should concentrate on. You can do this by drawing a circle around the cell a pupil has numbered (or by using a highlighter pen) as shown below.

	Y6 (1)	Y6 (2)	Y7 (1)	Y7 (2)
I can describe the pattern in my results.	④	①		

In the example shown above the pupil has identified that they feel very confident in this aspect but you feel there is still some work to be done.

5   Now the teacher should write one concise *diagnostic* statement in the teacher's box at the bottom of the sheet for each aspect highlighted. In the example shown above in step four you might write 'Sometimes ... (name of pupil) gets confused with the order of numbers in the pattern' or '... (name of pupil) has a problem relating change in one thing to change in another'.

6   Select one piece from the bridging work that represents good perform-ance or effort in relation to one or more aspects on the record. This should be no more than one double-sided sheet of A4. Pupils should have some involvement, under the teacher's guidance, in what work is chosen. Staple the pupil's work to the record sheet.

7   Now store the records for transfer to the secondary school.

Instructions provided for Y7 teachers

1   Read the record sheets transferred from the primary schools for pupils in your class before you teach the bridging lessons. Pay particular atten-tion to the aspects highlighted by the Y6 teacher and her/his diagnostic comments.

2   Towards the end of the bridging lessons, give pupils back their self-review sheets and ask them to review their performance again using col-umn three. (The same guidance, as in point number four above for Y6 teachers, was provided for Y7 teachers.)

3   Collect individual records and read them.

4   On each pupil's sheet, highlight up to three aspects that you think the pupil should concentrate on now. You can do this by drawing a circle around the printed one that the child has numbered (or by using a high-lighter pen).

5   Now write one concise *diagnostic* statement in the Y7 teachers' box at the bottom of the sheet for each aspect you have highlighted.

6 Give the sheets back to the pupils.
7 You can repeat the process towards the end of Y7 so that pupils (and you) can track further progression and identify additional targets for improvement.

Thus the record required pupils to self-review their progress but with a facility for the teacher to check the accuracy of pupils' ratings and to provide a diagnostic comment on progress that should help secondary teachers plan interventions accordingly. In this way the system avoided criticisms that the information transferred, typically just the National Curriculum level or test mark achieved for science, does not help teachers take actions that meet individual needs.

Logistics of document transfer mean that, however carefully systems are designed, many secondary teachers (sometimes quite justifiably) still claim they do not receive all records from new pupils arriving in their classes. To avoid this, the LA in York arranged a collection scheme whereby each primary school's records were collected before the end of the summer term in envelopes coded with the names of secondary schools to which pupils would transfer. These envelopes were sorted into boxes and delivered into the hands of the head of science at each of the receiving secondary schools. The same scheme was used to collect and transfer work in English and mathematics. The whole process was completed before the end of the summer term so that teachers in secondary schools would have time to look at the records for pupils entering their classes in September of the new school year.

Did the scheme work?

In evaluation of the STAY bridging project, teachers were asked how they found using the assessment and transfer record. Twenty-one primary teachers in schools teaching the Fizzy Drinks unit, described in Chapter 6, were interviewed by telephone. The detailed methodology is described elsewhere (see Braund, 2007). Most teachers (19/21) said they had used the scheme and thought it was a good idea. There was some concern, however, that pupils were unsure of the method of assessment (6/21) or that they tended to overrate their capabilities when completing the form (9/21). Here are three typical responses:

> Yes, they (pupils) had to think back – difficult at the start (of the bridging work) to think back. I'd say they were sometimes over-enchanted with what they can do and are not used to this process.

> I could see the point but we need to be doing it earlier in KS2 as pupils couldn't self-assess realistically.

> No! They (the pupils) didn't like it. Some were honest – the ones who said they were hopeless at things. I'm not convinced by this ... we had a very rushed half-term.

As described previously, the assessment scheme drew heavily on suggestions made by Black and Wiliam (1998). In their later work, however, Black and Wiliam recognize that self-assessment is hard to use properly when pupils do not also engage in peer assessment (for example, by working in pairs) or do not understand the criteria by which they are required to rate their abilities (Black et al, 2002). From informal discussions with teachers, it seems that both of these had occurred. In addition, this scheme was used at a time when formative and diagnostic systems were only just beginning to feature in the lexicon of primary practice, although secondary schools in the study were more used to the principles through Key Stage 3 Strategy training.

As described in Chapter 6, the views of secondary school teachers continuing the scheme were collected by co-ordinators responsible for KS3 teaching in each school. All nine secondary schools confirmed they had received assessment transfer record sheets from primary schools, showing that the transfer procedure worked, yet only two said they continued the pupils' self-review scheme into Y7. While some co-ordinators said teachers found work brought from KS2 of use (3), others (4) felt that transferred information did not help them progress pupils' levels in process skills. The comments below represent these two views.

> Teachers in our school thought it was interesting to see what had been done and it did give an idea about the standard of the pupils' work. However, time limitations meant that staff were not able to go through each pupil's work.

> There was a lack of consistency in what we got from primary schools. Some sheets were just ticked by the pupils to say what they thought they could do. Only a few of the sheets contained a comment from the teacher – so it was no help to us really.

The scheme was used one year later when the Fizzy Drinks unit was taught in a further eight schools feeding one secondary school in the East Riding of Yorkshire. Here the last type of comment above was rare. It seemed that primary teachers had provided extensive diagnostic comments. Despite this, receiving teachers in the secondary school still seemed to ignore the record.

Taking on board these concerns, the assessment scheme was simplified for teaching the Bread unit in the second year of the STAY project in York schools. In this version pupils were not required to self-assess, rather teachers were simply asked to rate each pupil against statements summarizing performance outcomes for competence in investigative skills such as planning, identifying patterns in data and suggesting conclusions. A second section required teachers to rate pupils' against expected outcomes for conceptual understanding. This revised scheme is provided as Text Box 8.2.

Interestingly, when teachers in 17 of the primary schools that had taught Fizzy Drinks were questioned following the teaching of the Bread unit one year later, a smaller proportion (12/17) said they had used this simplified scheme. It was noticeable that teachers using the original scheme were far

Text Box 8.2

Simplified transfer record used in the second year of the STAY project

Name _____

School _____

Please tick next to the most appropriate expectation statement.

In terms of scientific enquiry

Please tick:	Expectations
	Some children will not have made so much progress and will: explain how they have made a fair comparison. Obtain and present results
	Most children will: plan an investigation that makes a fair comparison. Obtain and present results in a way that helps to show patterns and draw conclusions
	Some children will have progressed further and will: present data as a line graph. Explain how their conclusions match the evidence obtained and suggest ways in which the data collected could be improved

In terms of life processes and living things

Please tick:	Expectations
	Some children will not have made so much progress and will: recognize that yeast is a very small living thing
	Most children will: recognize that yeast can feed, grow and reproduce like other living things
	Some children will have progressed further and will: describe evidence that yeast is living and explain why yeast is affected by temperature

Optional teacher's comments:

more likely than those using the simplified version a year later to identify specific skills in which their pupils had improved as a result of carrying out bridging work. In year 1 of the project process skills such as commenting on reliability of results (8/21), controlling variables (7/21), planning investigations (5/21) and graphing (5/21) were all mentioned. When using the simplified scheme in year 2, teachers rarely referred to progress in these process skills. It seems that while the revised scheme may have been easier to use, it did not provide the detailed level of assessment needed to identify competence and progression in relation to process skills in science.

So the revised assessment and transfer record seems to have fallen short in terms of its usefulness to teachers. It seems there is a gap between the rhetoric expressed by some secondary teachers, bemoaning the quality of transferred assessment in helping them plan and teach for progression, and what they are prepared to do with this level of information when they actually get it. Too much information is unusable and too little is not useful. This conundrum remains a key issue in transition work but is not one that the project teams at York have been able to solve. This is not to say that schemes like those shown here are not worth using. It is interesting to speculate that the original self-review and diagnostic scheme might find more acceptance now as schools come on board with ideas and procedures concerned with formative and diagnostic assessment. This is certainly borne out by findings of school inspections (Ofsted, 2006: para. 226, 55) though more noticeably for English and mathematics than in science.

The ASE science passport

Before leaving the area of recording and reporting progress in science across the primary–secondary transfer it is worth reporting another widely used initiative. In an effort to promote science and technology, and in particular science education, 2002 was dedicated 'science year' in the UK. As part of this initiative a plethora of resources to help science teachers was produced by the Association for Science Education (ASE). The ASE produced a series of CDs containing learning activities such as interactive games, practical activities and text- related tasks for pupils. Materials to be used directly by the teacher included ideas to enhance pupil progression across the KS2/3 transfer (ASE, 2002; www.sycd.co.uk/). On one of these CDs, 'Who am I?', a *pupils' passport* was provided, designed as a template to record successful bridging activity between primary and secondary schools. The idea of the passport was that it can be used as an activity in Y6 and Y7 to help pupils focus on their investigative (process) skills and to record achievements. Essentially the passport offers a start in the transition process through a choice of investigations and structured follow-up. The intention is that Y6 teachers issue pupils with colour or black and white copies of passports and pupils collect 'visas' (icons) awarded by the teacher to mark achievement in scientific skills. Achievement 'visas' can be awarded by the teacher using their own criteria or can be tied to suggested investigations that can be started in Y6 and continued after transfer. The passport idea therefore acts as a stand-alone transfer record or can be part of more structured bridging like that described in other chapters of this book. Investigations suggested for bridging include:

- *Looking at habitats and adaptations*. The amount of fieldwork required is flexible and options for studying different habitats mean that school geography is not a barrier. Communication, group work and literacy are highlighted at different points in the activity.
- *Solutions*. This uses dissolving jelly as a focus for developing investigative and practical skills, including prediction, analysis and evaluation.
- *Golden ratio*. Focusing on their faces, pupils collect variation data that draws them into the world of the ancient Greek Golden Ratio. Numeracy is highlighted in the calculation of simple ratios (ASE, 2002).

In addition, pupils can add to their passports details of equipment, vocabulary and ICT resources used, including websites visited. The passport provides opportunities to collect personal data that can be used as part of investigations into human variation and some questions that probe pupils' beliefs about the nature of science.

Comparing standards across transfer: towards a more productive system?

I have pointed out in this chapter and elsewhere in this book that the issue of comparability of standards either side of primary–secondary transfer is a contentious and controversial one. Yet, according to the literature, considering samples of pupils' work is something that commonly features in liaison meetings between primary and secondary teachers (Galton et al., 2003b; Stillman and Maychell, 1984). It even seems that teachers are disappointed when such exercises are not included at these events (Suffolk Education Department, 1996). Unfortunately these meetings often involve unproductive haranguing when teachers refuse to accept each others' judgements based on National Curriculum levels because of the reasons I discussed previously and in Chapter 4. So project teams at York decided to use a different system to compare standards. We applied our system for pupils' work connected with procedural knowledge (assessment of process skills) as that was the focus of the bridging work described in Chapter 6.

First, rather than teachers just turning up ad hoc with their pupils' work, we collected or asked teachers to send us samples of work connected with practical investigations ahead of liaison meetings. The work we asked for might be whole accounts of investigations, statements concerned with predictions or conclusions, graphs, tables of results, and so on. We asked for samples of work from beyond just the classes either side of transfer (Years 6 and 7), thus assuring wider views of progression across the adjacent key stages. For example, we asked teachers from primary schools to give us samples of work from Years 4, 5 and 6 and secondary teachers to give us work from Years 7, 8 and 9. The team anonymized work, removing pupils' names and the year groups to which samples belonged. We ascribed a letter code to each sample recording for ourselves to which year group each example belonged. At the liaison meetings we placed teachers in primary–secondary pairings wherever possible and provided work that we knew represented a range of ages either side of transfer, typically work from either Y4 and from Y5 or Y6 and from Y7 and Y8 or Y9. Instead of using the contentious and often inadequate level descriptions published in the National Curriculum documents, we asked teachers to consider each piece of work according to an aide-memoire describing desirable attributes of quality work in scientific enquiry. Taken together, the list of attributes represents a rather daunting list. If the attributes were to be achieved collectively then the student would probably be signing up for advanced study, but they are not intended to be used holistically. The aide-memoire is provided as Text Box 8.3

Below is the sequence that we used in liaison meetings to help teachers talk about samples of work.

1   Working in pairs or groups of three or four, teachers used the aide-memoire (Text Box 8.3) to assess each of the samples of pupils' work provided for targeted process skills in science. We decided in advance which skills were most appropriate to judge for each sample.
2   Teachers identified and agreed, for each piece of work, the process skill that they would concentrate on if giving the pupil formative feedback. This provided us with a consistent way of reinforcing the value of formative assessment discussed earlier in this chapter.
3   Teachers noted, for each piece of work, what year group they thought each piece of work was from (for example, Y5, Y6, Y7, Y8, Y9). We expected teachers to be able to justify their choices.
4   We asked teachers to choose one piece of work from the samples provided and one process skill, and to write on the work (in red pen if desired) one comment giving precise diagnostic and formative feedback on how this pupil applied/used the targeted process skill and what they would have to do in the future to further develop this skill. In this way we reinforced the formative, 'next steps' approach valued in Black and Wiliam's work discussed earlier.
5   Finally we revealed the actual year group to which samples of pupils' work belonged.

In one instance, when using this approach, we touched on a few, very 'raw nerves'. When we revealed the actual year group of pupils' work, two secondary teachers flatly refused to believe that an example was produced by a pupil

---

Text Box 8.3

Quality and Capability in Scientific Enquiry – an Aide-Memoire

- How clear is the enquiry question – does it refer to both the independent and dependent variables?
- Is there a clear description of what the scientific enquiry is about?
- Does the pupil make a prediction that gives a reason?
- Does the prediction include a sketch graph of the expected relationship between the variables?
- Is a fair-test approach adopted?
- Does the pupil choose an appropriate range for, interval between, and number of values of the independent variable in a fair-test investigation?
- Does the pupil take repeated measurements and work out the mean?
- Are the results presented in a suitable table?
- Is the pattern in the results identified and described clearly?
- Is evidence related to scientific knowledge?
- Does the pupil evaluate how easy or difficult it was to make the test fair?
- Is there an evaluation of the accuracy of measurements?
- Does the pupil evaluate the reliability of the results?
- Are there any suggestions for further enquiry?

---

from Y6. Unbeknown to the team managing the meeting, that pupil's teacher was present and declared to the meeting that this was indeed work from her Y6 class. Both secondary teachers continued to challenge the work, claiming that it must be atypical of the standards in her Y6 class. When the primary teacher replied that this work was actually of average quality and that she could have chosen even better work, the secondary teachers then claimed her school must be one that was particularly advantaged. The primary teacher then pointed out of the window of the training centre in which the meeting was held saying, 'that is my school over there – it is in the middle of the most disadvantaged part of the borough – are you satisfied now?' The coda to this story is that, at the time of the meeting, performance data for the LA in which the training took place showed primary schools above the national average for performance at KS2 in science while secondary performance at GCSE was among the worst for England. It is no surprise to say that this meeting helped spark huge investment to raise standards in teaching in secondary schools in this particular LA.

Chapter summary

Few secondary teachers trust the standards and levels in science at which pupils entering secondary school are said to be at. Assessment information and records are infrequently used to guide progress after transfer. Teams at York devised a formative and progressive scheme involving pupils in self-assessment of their process skills. While this attempt was valued, particularly by primary teachers, it was not often continued in secondary schools. It seems that too much information is unusable and too little is not useful. The ASE pupils' passport provides a transfer record that can be used in stand-alone transfer systems or can be connected to bridging work. Liaison meetings are useful ways of tackling the issue of progression across transfer, although using National Curriculum levels is less productive than using other criteria that reinforce the usefulness of formative and diagnostic feedback to help pupils progress.

Suggested actions

- Use the aide-memoire and procedures suggested in this chapter at liaison meetings of teachers to look at pupils' work.
- Consider using or adapting systems like the ASE's pupil passport to help value the work that pupils have done at primary school. Use it to recognize what equipment and scientific vocabulary has been previously used in the primary school.
- Decide what actual examples of pupils' work will be sent to the secondary school. Secondary teachers should always try to refer to at least some examples of the work received and show a real interest in it.

9

Sharing Practice

with Celia Moore

Chapter overview

Three activities that teachers can engage in to share and understand each other's practice are described: co-planning, co-observation and co-teaching. Protocols, criteria and methods that allow high-quality, productive observations of teaching are included.

There is consensus, according to evaluations of projects addressing transfers and transitions, that those that worked best and had longest-lasting impact involved co-operation and co-working where sharing and understanding each other's practice played a key role. This applies equally to projects addressing general, social aspects of primary–secondary transfer and those focused on specific subjects like science (Suffolk Education Department, 1996; Suffolk County Council Education Department, 2002a; 2002b). Co-operation aimed at establishing better understanding of each other's teaching methods and styles addresses the fourth and, some would argue the most important, of Galton's four 'bridges' described in Chapters 2 and 5, that is, addressing curriculum and pedagogy. In a review of KS2/3 transfer projects in science funded by the AZSTT, Bishop and Denley (2003: 9) asserted that: 'It is teachers collaborating, sharing and reflecting jointly on experiences of teaching and learning science that is most likely to lead to pedagogical change and a consequent harmonisation of approaches'.

Three areas of co-working between schools and teachers are considered here along with effects on the development of cross-phase understanding of science teaching and learning:

- co-planning
- co-observation
- co-teaching.

Co-planning of science work

Examples of co-planned, sometimes co-taught, work relating specifically to bridging were discussed in Chapters 6 and 7. At a simpler, less-involved level, just viewing each other's schemes of work at joint meetings of teachers is one way of establishing conversations about what is learned at adjacent key stages.

Some suggestions for jointly planned work, however, seem overambitious or even downright implausible. For example, in their book on primary–secondary transition, Nicholls and Gardner suggest that Y6 and Y7 teachers should jointly agree the content to be taught in each year and plan their teaching programmes accordingly (Nicholls and Gardner, 1999: 69). While the aim of improving progression and continuity for pupils learning science is a laudable one, surely this goes beyond what is practical.

To make joint planning activity effective and avoid problems it is important to revisit first principles, namely, relationships between participant teachers. Meetings where joint discussions about teaching and learning take place will, almost by definition, have an impact on professional relationships. One would hope this impact would be positive. Of significant importance is secondary teachers having a good understanding of what has been taught, and how, during the primary phase. It is also crucial that the primary teachers see that secondary colleagues value their work rather than are dismissive of it. Primary teachers have often not qualified in science subjects and can feel vulnerable when teaching such a subject. They then might feel like second-class citizens and, like their pupils, feel that secondary schools contain the real science experts and call all the shots anyway.

A group of schools that Celia Moore worked with in South Wales recognized this as a problem and challenged themselves to do something about it. A member of the secondary school leadership team was given specific responsibility for transfer, transition and liaison. The head teacher delegated responsibility while maintaining an overview. Significantly, the assistant head teacher was given time and a small budget to enable the work to develop. Initial contacts with primary schools were quite low key with the assistant head teacher from the secondary school merely asking to sit in on Year 6 lessons; markedly different from the more detailed lesson observations described later in this chapter. She wanted to get a flavour of what was taught and how it was taught, in a totally non-judgemental way. It was also an opportunity to get to know pupils and for them to get to know a member of staff who would soon become very important to them at their next school. This happened in all of the secondary school's feeder (primary) schools throughout the school year starting in September. Time was a critical factor, as with most things in school. However, knowing that this was supported by all the head teachers in the family of (feeder primary) schools was a real fillip for all staff involved in this process.

Once teachers had established good working relationships, they entered into constructive dialogue about transition practices in general and decided that they would make science a focus for their initial work. Primary and secondary teachers met together, discussed options and worked up a scheme of practical science lessons to be taught in the secondary school that would support primary pupils leading up to the end of Key Stage 2 SATs (the project was initially set up before KS2 SATs became optional in Wales in 2005). Pupils in Y5 visited the secondary school after Y6 had taken their SATs and visits continued through to their own end of key stage SATs one year later. In Year 5 the pupils studied living things followed by materials and their properties in the autumn term and light in the spring term. Pupils were very engaged in their learning, using appropriate scientific language and seemed generally more interested in science than in previous years. This helped to make revision for SAT tests at the primary school less of a chore. The arrangement added value for pupils and teachers because primary pupils were taught in laboratories and therefore became familiar with the location of the science department, safety and other school rules. Pupils were subsequently able to start practical science as soon as they moved to the secondary school without the need for another round of lessons on the Bunsen burner and making safety rules posters.

As visits took place every five or six weeks this enabled relationships to develop. The class teacher and a teaching assistant accompanied the pupils on visits; thus the 'getting to know you' phase took place in a very supportive environment. Primary teachers valued being part of the lessons and cross-phase pedagogic knowledge was generated almost incidentally and in a collegiate, hands-on way. Secondary teachers were able to build up their knowledge of the pupils, their particular needs and foibles which all ensured a good start to science when pupils eventually transferred. When Year 6 had completed all their visits, and their end of key stage tests, the head of science attended an assembly in each primary school to award individual pupil certificates. This was seen as a rite of passage and pupils were proud and pleased to have their achievements recognized in this way.

 Reflection

Discuss the advantages and disadvantages of working on liaison projects such as the one described above.

Co-observation of science lessons

The process

According to a systematic review of international research on the impact of collaborative continuing professional development (CPD) for teachers, an essential element of successful schemes is that they provide chances for co-observation of teaching. Indeed, it appears that schemes having low impact often lack this (Cordingley et al., 2003). In a survey of transfer projects shortly after the introduction of the National Curriculum in 1989, it was found that personal contacts, cross-phase visits and observations were all valued more highly by teachers than meetings to discuss documentation, schemes of work or assessment (Lee et al., 1995). With the introduction of the Key Stage Strategy in 2000, and its emphasis on KS2/3 transfer, the frequency of observations of teaching in primary schools by secondary teachers has grown rapidly. However, perhaps as a result of priorities for developing literacy and numeracy at the time, observations were confined mainly to English and mathematics, and were rarely in science lessons (Ofsted, 2002b). Since 2002 the science part of the Key Stage 3 Strategy has recommended and has provided funding for observation of primary science by secondary teachers. Since most of the funding went to secondary schools for them to develop their science teaching, it seemed that, unless secondary schools donated some of this funding, primary teachers were left out of the equation and, so, rarely got to see teaching in secondary schools. This was a situation that project teams at York were able to change by allocating funds directly to primary schools. Over four years of the projects the following took place:

- Thirteen project teachers involved in writing the bridging materials described in Chapter 5 watched each other teaching a lesson from the unit they developed in the alternate key stage to the one in which they usually taught. A member of the project team visited each project school to debrief and record outcomes.
- Secondary teachers in the nine high schools that agreed to teach the Fizzy Drinks unit observed teaching of bridging lessons in their local feeder primary schools. This was funded as part of the KS3 Strategy in the City of York.
- All primary schools in the City of York were contacted and offered funding equivalent to one half-day of supply cover to allow a Y6 (or other) teacher to observe teaching of secondary science. At the end of the autumn term, 11 out of the 49 primary schools had taken up this opportunity. Funding was provided by the AZSTT.
- All nine teachers involved in writing the Scientific Enquiry Progression Tasks (SEPTs – discussed in Chapter 7) as part of the North Yorkshire AstraZeneca Science Pedagogy and Progression (NYASPP) project co-observed and in some cases co-taught lessons in their cluster schools and sometimes in schools which had not been involved in preparing the materials. These teachers were interviewed and their reflections on observations recorded verbatim.

The teams at York drew on research on best practice in co-observation of teaching to avoid some of the pitfalls previously identified with this type of professional development. We also wanted to avoid situations where atypical science teaching was set up especially for visits (Galton et al., 2003a). Rather, our aim was to provide mechanisms and the space to allow a professionally useful dialogue by way of what Schön has called reflection in practice (Schön, 1983; 1987). To promote such dialogue we advised that:

1   Observations require a focus, for example on teachers' questioning, the organization of practical work, pupils' group discussion skills, and so on. Lack of focus has been identified as a feature of failed attempts to get teachers to discuss aspects of good practice in transfer work (Stillman and Maychell, 1984) or for establishing an understanding of why teachers act in the ways they do in different classroom environments (Galton et al., 2003b).

2   What is recorded should be factual or framed as questions to discuss rather than being judgemental about the teaching or the teacher observed. This avoids confusing the types of classroom observation required here with those that teachers might have experienced elsewhere, for example, to assess teachers' capability or competence, through appraisal or during training (Cosh, 1999).

3   The lesson observed must be discussed by observer and observee. Teachers were advised to talk through the lesson immediately after the observation or as soon after it as was possible. Some did this by telephone, but a face-to-face meeting was always preferred. We advised that observations should be shared and discussed in a way that focused on important features of the teaching and what children learned, that is, a *professional dialogue* about teaching and learning science. School inspections reveal that too often observations fail to get to grips with key issues as they end without sufficient discussion of teaching approaches and lesson outcomes (Ofsted, 2002b).

4   Records and notes of observations should be left with the teacher observed. Nothing should be taken away unless this has been mutually agreed (for example, samples of children's work, and so on). If teachers wanted to reflect on what they had each learned at a later date, then we advised them to agree how this was to be done before they left.

To provide a framework for co-observations and to facilitate quality in ensuing discussions in the alternate key stage, teams at York developed a special pro forma. This is provided as Text Boxes 9.1 and 9.2.

The pro forma has sides A and B. On side A, teachers were advised to record what was seen and noticed. Side B was reserved for reflection. In the boxes on both sides, questions were provided to focus observations and reflections more onto key aspects of teaching and learning that are particularly relevant to science lessons likely to be seen across the KS 2/3 transfer. It is our view that these questions would apply equally well to other transfer and transition points, and so the pro forma has wider use. In line with advice discussed earlier, we encouraged teachers to select a particular focus for observations – so it was not always necessary for them to complete every section of the forms.

The extent to which teachers actually played a participant role during observation was a matter of personal choice, though we took Peter Wood's view that good ethnographic study relies on participant observation, as there is no substitute for understanding the experiences of others unless you can

---

Text Box 9.1

SIDE A: Observing teaching and learning of science in an alternate key stage

Lesson title/aim _____

Children working:

What was the balance between independent and directed work? How did the teacher encourage children to think for themselves? How were children encouraged to raise their own questions?

Organization and monitoring:

How does the organization of the learning environment facilitate practical work for science? How is support, challenge and target-setting used within groups and for individuals?

Language and questioning:

How were questions used to help children think and take decisions? How were children focused on specific demands of process skills? How did the teacher's language and phrasing (e.g. of questions) used in this lesson compare with your own?

---

have a go yourself (Woods, 1986: 33). For example in many cases teachers chose to talk with children so that they could see how learning related to the planned objectives for the lesson. We advised, however, that quality participant observation relies on being unobtrusive. The role is therefore one of a friendly *participant observer* with an interest in the teaching *and* learning taking place, not one of being an extra or assistant teacher.

Text Box 9.2

SIDE B: Reflecting on teaching and learning of science in an alternate key stage

Lesson title/aim _____ _____

Outcomes:

Did the children learn what was expected of them? If not, what were the problems they had? How did the standard of their work compare with that which you would normally expect from the children you teach?

Differentiation:

How did the classroom organization and teaching support children who found the learning challenging? How did it challenge the most able children? How were targets set for individuals and groups, e.g. for completion, improvement, relating to expectations, etc.?

Timing/pace:

How did concentration times and the time children took to complete tasks compare with the classes you teach? How quickly did the children respond to the demands of tasks? What did the teacher do to move from one phase of the lesson to the next? How did the organization and timing within the lesson compare with the way that you normally pace and organize a science lesson?

〰 **Reflection**

Discuss how the methods of co-observation described compare with other examples of lesson observation that you have been involved in.

Teachers' reflections

Project team members followed up most of the co-observations of teaching described above. The completed observation pro formas and particularly transcriptions of interviews held in schools are a rich source of data. Responses frequently showed the deep level of professional insights gained. There is not the space here to do full justice to these studies, but perhaps it is worth looking at just one pair of teachers, Cath (a primary teacher and Greta (a secondary teacher) who watched each other's teaching as part of the development of a NYASPP unit called 'Mouldy Old Dough' (see Chapter 7). Here is what Greta said after watching Cath's lesson in the primary school.

> In some ways Cath teaches very much like I teach. She set the scene which the students could relate to, which was the story of her daughter leaving a cup under the bed and finding a mouldy old sandwich there. She used more scientific language than I would have expected such as talking about the *independent* and *dependent* variables. We (in secondary schools) also need to make sure that the language we use is the same in primary school and secondary school ... and there are times when we don't do that. Like in *CASE* teaching we have *input* and *outcome* words to describe variables in an investigation – it matters to the children – we are confusing them. Cath's questions are very open ended. There is no 'yes', or 'no' answers. She encourages thinking skills and with my *CASE* stuff we are doing the same. (Greta, Tillham Grammar School, May 2004)

From this I think it is clear that Greta recognized continuity in teaching methods and so was pleased to see ways that Cath contextualized her teaching and developed pupils' thinking skills. Greta mentions CASE (Cognitive Acceleration in Science Education; Adey et al. 1989). This is a commonly used scheme in secondary schools in the UK. The CASE teaching involves special lessons taught at two-weekly intervals among normal teaching. The aim of CASE is to develop, specific aspects of reasoning such as proportionality, control of experimental variables and correlation through a variety of structured tasks. It has been claimed that CASE teaching develops general cognitive abilities that can be applied to and help advance thinking in science but that have applications to and help raise performance in other school subjects (Adey and Shayer, 1994). Greta recognizes that the language Cath uses to talk to her pupils about experimental variables, *independent* and *dependent* variables, is inconsistent with terms used for these same things in CASE teaching, respectively *input* and *output*. Greta recognizes the problems that this might cause for her pupils following transfer.

Cath, the primary teacher, was asked to say what she thought about the ways in which Greta used questions in the secondary school lesson she observed. Since Cath was also interested in developing a CASE approach to science teaching in her primary school, this aspect was of particular interest to her.

It was excellent. Because I had been involved in CASE lessons in my own school. Watching Greta do it has made me much more aware of not always asking the questions and asking the group. Things like 'has anyone got that too?', and 'would anyone like to ask that group a question about what they found out?'. It's quite interesting asking the children to do much more, referring back to the children rather than you always making a direct observation about things that happened. So rather than me saying 'is that always true?', it's like saying, 'would anyone like to ask that group a question?'. That's probably the biggest difference in our teaching. Greta's questions were all open-ended. (Cath, Walmdale Primary School, June 2004)

These sorts of reflections on subtle yet important differences in pedagogical approaches were common in our discussions with teachers and give us great hope that, despite the efforts in time and cost in setting up this type of teacher interchange, these actions will be crucial to understanding each other's classrooms.

Co-teaching

In the NYASPP project described in Chapter 7, some of the teachers designing progression units decided to co-teach in the alternative key stage to the one in which they normally taught. So the primary teacher taught in Y7 and the secondary teacher taught in Y6. In one writing pair, 'Lighting Up' – on electrical circuits, the teachers taught their unit to classes in schools that had not been involved in trials of the units. In effect this was co-teaching in the cold, a rather brave thing to attempt, but it seemed to generate some deep insights on teaching and learning. The secondary teacher involved, Bob, describes how co-teaching was organized.

Jason, the Year 6 class teacher at Holdsworth, did the lesson. He did the first hour which was the Scientific Enquiry Progression Task (SEPT) and then I took over, which is what the deal was going to be ... if he did the first hour I'd take over when it came to the investigation bit. Kate (the primary teacher that helped write the task) came as well so there were three of us and there were two support staff because there were two kids who were autistic.

Later, during interview, Bob described his reactions to ways in which pupils at the primary school were organized for and engaged in group discussions:

What was really impressive, what impressed us both, was the way kids could sit around a table and discuss things with each other and listen to each other. Our kids (in Y7) can't and yet these are Year 6 kids who were sitting and listening to each other and they had rules for listening and rules for debate and they knew them. They only had to have one little word (from the teacher), 'remember how we do this', and they came up with one or two key words and they just did it. Jason (the Y6 teacher) said, 'I've done this deliberately because I want the brighter ones to lead on'. So me and Kate thought ... well this is peer teaching ... and it was good. We were amazed that for two hours kids were on task.

Towards the end of his interview, Bob reflected on the relative freedoms and competence of pupils in primary science teaching compared with that in his own school:

I would have thought they (the teachers) would have been more tightly focused in primary than they were. They weren't. They let the kids do a lot more. We keep saying we will do all this (in secondary schools) and you know, my God, they are doing it more than we do!

Bob is an experienced science teacher, a head of science, confident and frequently involved in curriculum innovations. I have seen his teaching many times and I know he often uses innovative and collaborative learning in his classroom. For such an experienced teacher to gain such deep insights on pupils' learning from co-teaching was surprising to me, but, ultimately I found it very refreshing. The benefits of teaching in each other's schools have been seen in other work, particularly in schools in Suffolk. It is claimed that this is particularly because standards of work, behaviour, organization and achievements are witnessed and experienced by teachers at first hand. Where this has been in addition to other liaison such as meetings, bridging and looking at assessed work, it is claimed benefits have been huge (Suffolk Education Department, 1996).

Perhaps it matters little as to what topics are taught and the precise methods used to share and understand each other's practice. As Celia Moore has said, good relationships and an atmosphere of professional trust are essential foundations for whatever is done. If these and other initiatives discussed here and elsewhere in this book help place transition on schools' agendas and improvement plans, then pupils will almost inevitably have a better experience as more staff will be aware of the issues and life will be better at the beginning of secondary school. Celia and I have often found that teachers generally like to work towards improving a subject area simply because in their minds, particularly at secondary school, their interest is in improving results in their subject and not about the development of the whole child. We are not saying this is wrong for it is a laudable aim yet, from these limited beginnings in one subject, it is our experience that growth can occur into a whole-school approach that can help develop each pupil's potential without compromising overall results and hence the league table status of the school.

Chapter summary

Good relationships between primary and secondary teachers help establish understanding and respect for different pedagogic approaches. As part of this it is important to establish protocols for the professional use of co-observation, and co-teaching. It is important that all teachers experience teaching in an alternate phase. Outcomes of co-observations show that pupils in primary schools work more independently and can achieve more than was previously thought possible. Co-observation and co-teaching also highlight the value of using language and scientific terms in consistent ways either side of transfer.

Suggested actions

- Provide opportunities for as many teachers as is possible to observe teaching in the alternate phase to the one in which they teach.
- Use the criteria, protocols and observation sheets to provide for professional reflection on co-teaching and co-observation of lessons.
- Consider teaching co-planned lessons in the alternate phase. This is most rewarding.

10

Better Progression and Continuity in Science: Implications for Practice

> ## Chapter overview
>
> This final chapter reviews the case for science learning as preparation for life. External cultural and policy changes influencing innovation and practices in schools are discussed. A number of institutional conditions likely to help projects be successful are provided.

Most of us would agree that a good start is desirable in new endeavours of our lives. In science, the realization that learning science in secondary schools and after other transfers is not new is a foundation on which good progress is made, yet in this book I have shown this is often ignored. Secondary schools offer options to 14-year-olds to study different subjects. Science subjects are not new to pupils, but the die (in terms of their attitudes) has often already been cast. Unless coerced or required to study sciences, most pupils would probably opt to do something else. This is waste on a grand scale: waste of individuals' potential, waste of potential scientists the economy needs, but more fundamentally, it represents disenfranchisement of a generation of youth. I discussed the importance of science education for scientific literacy in Chapter 3 and there are many other important reasons for learning science that I have described elsewhere (for example, Braund and Reiss, 2006). If we turned out pupils from our schools who were illiterate and innumerate there would rightly be public outrage, but how many would express indignation at the lack of knowledge of the atom, of DNA, of particle theory or the mechanisms that have shaped and might secure the future of our planet? Sometimes it seems that ignorance or disinterest in science is worn as a badge of honour. How many television quiz shows have you watched where the quizmaster or participants moan at the announcement of the 'science round'? As has often been quoted, 'knowledge is power' but for science why should we accept another saying, that 'ignorance is bliss'. I admit that some science is hard. I find it difficult to grasp ideas about circuit electricity, energy and even DNA replication and gene transfers (though I have a background in biology). Being bothered to make the mental effort to understand is only part of the story, although I suspect there is now more of a tendency towards mental apathy as far as some science subjects are concerned. Far more dangerous would be an inability to engage with matters that determine most of what is going on around us. It is not only this lack of understanding much science that is dangerous but an implicit trust in the word of the scientist 'as expert witness' that worries me most. How often do you notice that people disengage when a so-called 'expert' pronounces on the discovery of x or why we should do y. He or she is 'expert' and must know what they are talking about and therefore can be trusted. So an ability to challenge the evidence base of claims made in the media will be increasingly important as will some knowledge and experience of the procedures through which that evidence is collected, tested and critiqued.

In this book I have presented and reviewed a number of methods to improve transfers and transitions in learning science. The final job then, is to discuss some of the conditions and influences under which these methods might flourish. I find it helpful to consider these in terms of an organizing framework (see Figure 10.1).

The framework has two layers, an outer one describing the external influences that have an impact and an inner one that describes some of the internal conditions at institutional level that I see as most likely to assure good practice in enhancing progression and continuity. These internal conditions are listed towards the end of the chapter, but first to the external factors.

External drivers

When I first conceived the framework shown as Figure 10.1, I placed 'External initiatives' (policies and practices) at the top of the diagram and 'External drivers' (society, culture and research) at the bottom. In doing this I became aware of falling into a trap of conventional thinking in education, that is, assuming that what is attempted and sometimes achieved by schools is solely determined by policies, initiatives and strategies originating from government. This is, of course, the reality in which many of us work, but it is important to realize that policies do not (or certainly in my opinion they should not) exist in a social and cultural vacuum. I consequently turned my framework on its head.

The changing culture of science education

I started this chapter by repeating the plea for science education as a literacy, a basic human and cultural right if you like, without which young people are disconnected and prevented from taking a full part in the society in which they

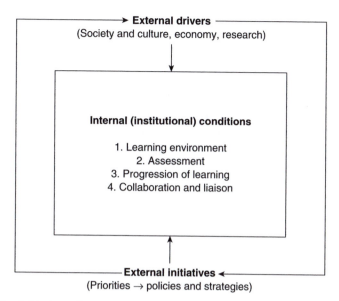

Figure 10.1   Initiatives, drivers and conditions determining policies and actions in improving progression and continuity in science learning

live. There is now at last a cultural shift in science education towards providing learning that is less driven by content and facts of sciences, more engaging for, and in tune with, the interests of young people and that provides the knowledge, skills and understanding of how scientists work that will hopefully provide the criticality necessary to challenge expert and media reporting of science.

The economic drivers of science

While we could say the culture of science education has shifted markedly in the last few years, economic imperatives requiring more scientists have been an issue for a century or more (Royal Society, 2006b). But now many countries are finding it even harder to recruit enough scientists and technologists as the impact of developing economies of Asia and the Far East increase competitiveness in the job market. Global supply and demand of personnel is just one aspect. There are now national imperatives in many countries of the West to at least maintain if not expand their scientific and commercial edge in generating new knowledge in sunrise technologies such as robotics, microelectronics, nanoscience, materials science, bio-informatics, gene therapies and so on. A supply of scientists in these endeavours requires young people to take an interest in science and for more of them to want to study it further and do it as a job.

Evidence-based policy and practice

In this book many of the methods described are promoted as being informed by research. This is part of a burgeoning culture in education towards selecting practices informed by, or based on, evidence of what works. Following actions in areas of social policy such as health, crime and justice and social care, education in many countries is moving towards developing professional practice grounded in sound evidence. This is what has come to be known as 'evidence-based' policy and practice. In UK education it grew out of fears in the mid-1990s that much educational research merely 'cluttered up journals that no one reads' rather than helping teachers and policy-makers take informed decisions on what might be best to do and ways of achieving it (Hargreaves, 1996: 4). Much of the evidence base that guides policy and practice comes from what are known as 'systematic reviews'. Typically all available research studies relevant to a particular question or problem are located and then sets of rigorous selection criteria are applied to narrow down the field to a few key studies that provide supposedly the 'best' (highest quality) evidence of effect. Since selection criteria are based on the paradigm of health science research where large-scale, randomized controlled trials (RCTs) – as in drug research – are a favoured method, this tends to set a quasi 'gold-standard' to which other studies are (often less favourably) compared. Thus smaller-scale, qualitative studies of, say, transfer arrangements in one cluster of schools and how they affect attitudes of boys and girls to science, are unlikely to make the cut as acceptable examples of high-quality research. This has led to criticism of how useful systematic reviews might be in helping teachers decide what is best at institutional and classroom level as so many studies on which published reports' findings are based seem too general and bland or lack the necessary detail on which to build specific teaching programmes that might have a chance of success. As a beginning teacher who looked at one report from a systematic review said:

> Education (for our group of novice teachers at least) is perhaps *nothing* like medicine. Muscle tissue absorbs the anti-inflammatory drug regardless of whether it is having a good day or not, whether it stayed up all night watching *Big Brother* or whether it missed breakfast. Chemical concentrations can be measured, responses of tissues to various stimulants may be reduced to simple reactions and quantified in the confines of a laboratory – but education deals with people – and people mobile in a society no less. To us, the nature of what works well in a classroom seemed far, far too messy to be summed up in statistics. Thus, the exclusion from the report (via the systematic sorting) of good qualitative data seemed disquieting. (Campbell et al., 2005: 9–10)

Another problem is that in research-based practice teachers, or more likely, head teachers, are looking for the 'big plus gains'. By this I mean research evidence that shows that intervention x will improve pupils' performance by a factor of y. A lot of educational research just does not show these sorts of gains. For example, the review of context-based learning of science discussed in a number of chapters in this book (Bennett et al., 2003) shows that pupils using these approaches are no better or worse at learning science (as judged by recall and application of science on conventional tests and examinations). But is this sufficient reason for not going down the context-led teaching route? There is other evidence, much of it discussed in this book, giving other and better reasons for doing so. If more motivated young people, more interested and engaged in science, is your goal rather than just examination results and league table status, then the decision has to be taken on a broader evidence base. This is why STAY project research teams provided a mixture of evidence to evaluate the bridging units discussed in Chapter 6. There is some quantitative evidence (by way of a limited RCT) that bridging units impact on pupils' performance in SAT questions about scientific procedures but to seize on this as the only important justification for using them would miss the point. For us at York it was the ways in which teaching using bridging units set whole-school agendas for tackling a number of issues at transfer that was important, as well as the performance gains evidenced through research.

Our experiences of bridging and many other initiatives and interventions have helped identify a number of 'conditions' under which transfer and transition arrangements for science might operate best, but first it is necessary to consider some of the policy and curriculum initiatives that are also important.

External initiatives and the curriculum dimension

There are two policy drivers that have affected science teaching and learning most either side of transfers. One is the way in which schooling has been organized and the other is the degree of convergence or divergence between ways in which science (and other subjects) has been structured and taught. The amount of change in both aspects in recent years has been unprecedented and, unfortunately, often steered more by political expediency than rational debate, research or reflection (see discussion of this in Braund, forthcoming).

The organization of schools

At the dawn of mass schooling at the end of the nineteenth century, most UK schools were organized on an all-age basis. There was no transfer from one school to another. This situation continued until the 1920s when the familiar landscape of primary (often separate infant and junior schools) and secondary schools emerged. With this new organization came the first realization that transition from one stage to another might be important. A seminal government report of the time (the Hadow report) stated that: 'There should be no sharp edges between infant, junior and post-junior stages and transition from one stage to the succeeding stage should be as smooth and gradual as possible' (cited in Stringer, 2003: 4–6).

In the 1960s and 1970s there were moves, in some regions of the UK, to address issues of progression and continuity through shifting the secondary transfer age to 13, 14 or even 15. Thus the concept of the 'middle school' was born. The thinking behind this was on two fronts. First, it was thought that pupils would be better prepared to tackle secondary school when they were more mature (especially boys) and, second, pupils would be more cognitively ready for the types of abstract thinking required in secondary schools. Thus the creation of middle schools owed much to the developmental psychology of Jean Piaget that had emerged and was influencing educational thinking and policy at that time. Since the introduction of the National Curriculum in 1989 the number of middle schools has declined markedly, largely as a result of the introduction of age-related key stages and national testing at 11 and 14. Secondary schools are less likely to want to receive pupils at 12 or 13 when they only have one or two years rather than three to teach material tested at the end of Key Stage 3 (age 14).

Interestingly, changes in teachers' pay and conditions in 1974 meant that more posts of responsibility were created in middle schools than in secondary schools to deal with transfers in and out of these schools. This is probably why Ofsted reported better transition arrangements and more sophisticated discussions between staff about pupils' work in middle schools than in secondary schools in Suffolk, an area that had retained middle schools (Suffolk Education Department, 1996). Recently a large-scale review of primary education in England has provided renewed support for the middle school concept:

> Interestingly, parents in a number of other soundings (carried out by the review team) commended a return to the middle school system to reduce the trauma of primary–secondary transfer and segregate younger children from the influence of teenagers. Contemporary anxieties are, in this case, prompting a desire to reinstate a pattern of schooling with which an earlier generation had decided to dispense. The middle schools may have disappeared but the anxieties have not, and for this reason we suggest that the issue is of much more than local interest. (Primary Review, 2007a: 39)

> There is a need to re-assess the case for the three-tier system of education, and for middle schools in particular, before they are finally phased out (a strong case for their retention was made on developmental grounds). (Primary Review, 2007b: 2)

As can be seen from these quotes, the grounds for reinstating middle schools are as much about behavioural influences as they are about teaching and learning though developmental arguments based on *Piagetian* stage-theory and are still strong. The middle school may yet prove to be a mode of organization that can offer much in addressing problems of progression and continuity in learning.

The organization of the curriculum in primary and secondary schools: divergence or convergence?

In the 1970s following the advent of comprehensive schools (see Glossary) there were a number of experiments to integrate subjects in the early years of secondary education. For example, history, geography, religious study, technology and, even, science might all be combined into one or two days devoted to a topic such as 'The Sea', 'Our changing world', 'The Earth', and so on (Stenhouse, 1971). Similar changes had taken place in primary schools. In the late 1960s the Plowden report (Central Advisory Council for Education, 1967) was seminal in changing primary school practice away from whole-class methods that had previously depended on drill and practice and rote learning to more child-centred approaches and informal activity-based learning. Post-Plowden, the practice became known as the 'integrated day' and was common in most schools. Typically pupils were placed into different activity-focused groups each pursuing work related to one or more curriculum area within a common topic such as 'Romans', 'Toys' and 'Our school' that acted as organizing frameworks for learning (Kerry and Eggleston, 1994). However, since subject integration in secondary schools was effectively very rare, and regarded with suspicion by many specialist subject teachers, parents and school governors, the pedagogy and practices of primary and secondary schools remained strongly divergent for at least 30 years.

Perhaps inevitably such liberalizing, child-centred moves in both primary and secondary sectors would elicit a response from the political right and in 1969 a series of educational 'Black Papers' were published (Cox and Dyson, 1969a; 1969b). Many facets of the 'new' curriculum and teaching methods in primary and secondary schools were attacked. For example, these developments in curriculum and pedagogy were seen as 'lowering standards' and the integrated day nothing more than 'inconsequential and unstructured play'. A further attack on the pedagogy of primary schools, a critique of progressive teaching, child-centred methods and integration of subject matter, occurred following the introduction of the National Curriculum in 1992. Concerned about so-called 'standards' in primary schools, John Major's Conservative government in 1991 established a review group comprising three eminent educators of the time to report on best practice in primary school organization and teaching. The so-called 'Three Wise Men's Report' that emerged claimed that the integrated, topic-based day and use of group work were ineffective in promoting the necessary degree of cognitive challenge required for pupils to progress (Alexander et al., 1992). The report criticized what it saw as the premise that subjects such as science, geography and particularly English and mathematics could contain suitable and sufficiently identifiable subject content (and so maintain their integrity) when constrained by and contained in a topic such as 'Romans', 'Toys', and so on. The report therefore promoted teaching of separate subjects using whole-class methods. Since the critique in this report appeared to reinforce the subject-based National Curriculum (although organization and teaching methods were never specified) the report was a key moment that changed practice in many primary schools. Thus primary practice now became much more like that of secondary schools, so much so that Galton's research team, replicating the 1976 ORACLE research 20 years later in 1996, speculated that transfer to secondary schools might no longer be the problem it once was (Hargreaves and Galton, 2002).

So what of the situation today? It seems that topic work and integration might be back on the agenda, at least in some parts of the UK. In 2007 Northern Ireland introduced a revised curriculum – rolled out for Years 1 and 5 – in which science moved from being a discrete subject to a contributory element, along with history, geography and technology, of a learning area called the 'world around us'. This area is divided into four strands: interdependence, place, movement and energy, and change over time. In Wales integration of science is not so noticeable, although increased emphasis on contextualization and how to teach rather than on what to teach is prominent. So an area called 'How things work' now includes some of the content previously taught as 'Forces' or as 'Electricity'. Contexts for teaching might be toys and devices found in the home. In Scotland there has been a national debate on education resulting in publication of *A Curriculum for Excellence*. At the heart of this is the aim of creating a seamless structure for learning from 3 to 18 that declutters content, encourages integration and *supports meaningful transitional practices*. There is a strong values-led element to the Scottish reforms, and hence aims to develop pupils as successful learners, confident individuals, responsible citizens and effective contributors to society. Coupled with this is a process whereby serving teachers can contribute to future development of the curriculum rather than receiving finished documents from a government agency – thus they contribute to 'a work in progress' (Primary Science Review, 2007).

It may be that, freed of the constraints of national testing, Scotland never had tests at 11 and Wales recently stopped them, as Northern Ireland will soon do, the countries of the UK other than England are moving towards a more adventitious and liberating curriculum. There are, however, significant changes on the horizon in England with publication of the largest review of primary education ever attempted, the *Primary Review* (whose first report was quoted earlier) and a radical new-look curriculum for Key Stage 3 to be introduced into all schools in 2008. The intention of curriculum 2008 (QCA, 2007a; 2007b) is to allow schools to concentrate more on key aspects of skills development and holistic learning (such as communication, collaboration and thinking skills) and consequently the subject content for science has been drastically reduced. The door is open for schools to integrate subjects if they so wish and we might speculate that, if this happens, similar moves might take place at Key Stage 2. A recent report on the effect of school size on learning suggests that small schools have an advantage when separate subject departments work together to integrate and co-ordinate their approaches to learning (Teach First, 2007). Thus it appears, for the time being, that there may be a period of divergence between primary and secondary schools followed again by some degree of convergence, but in a different direction to before – once again towards more child-centred learning.

The internal (institutional) conditions for better progression and continuity

A study of the world's top-performing school systems (for example, Taiwan, Singapore, Hong Kong, Australia and Japan) shows they share three essential features:

- teachers recruited from the highest qualified graduates
- high-quality and sustained professional development
- ensuring high-quality instruction for all learners (Barber and Mourshed, 2007).

The study went on to show that all three of these interact and must be concurrent. Barber and Mourshed suggest three conditions most likely to make this happen:

1   Individual teachers need to become aware of specific weaknesses in their own practice. In most cases, this not only involves building an awareness of what they do but the mindset underlying it.
2   Individual teachers need to gain understanding of specific best practices. In general, this can only be achieved through the demonstration of such practices in an authentic setting.
3   Individual teachers need to be motivated to make the necessary improvements. In general, this requires a deeper change in motivation that cannot be achieved through changing material incentives. Such changes come about when teachers have high expectations, a shared sense of purpose, and above all, a collective belief in their common ability to make a difference to the education of the children they serve. (Barber and Mourshed, 2007: 27)

So realization of the problem, an understanding of best practice and teachers' shared motivation to make necessary changes have a pay-off in good instruction and, consequently, better pupil performance. This would seem to be especially true for addressing progression and continuity at key transition points in learning because of the multifaceted nature of the problems and the need for co-ordinated approaches. A lot of resources (financial as well as time) have been put into initiatives to improve transitions and transfers particularly at the primary–secondary interface. Experience and evidence from research shows that where these have failed to match expectations this has been because:

- not enough time has been provided for initiatives, interventions and teaching to become embedded in teachers' practice (Ofsted 2002b; Peacock, 1999)

- the foci of initiatives has been too wide and involved too many schools (Peacock, 1999)
- not enough support from LA staff, for example, advisory teachers, was provided to help implementation at school level (Schagen and Kerr, 1999).

One of the problems threatening change of practice in UK schools has been the sheer volume of initiatives that teachers have had to deal with. In just the past three years or so there have been major changes at a number of levels affecting curriculum, pedagogy, child welfare, behavioural management, school attendance, drug and alcohol abuse, healthy eating, and so on. There seems to be an inherent assumption in England today that schools must be challenged to meet any problem that society throws up. Children neglected and abused – integrate child welfare with education; increasing teenage pregnancy – more sex-education; global warming – teach ESD (Education for Sustainable Development); not enough people voting – teach citizenship. The list goes on. As the plethora of programmes to tackle society's ills increases, financial and political incentives for schools are also changing. Some of these changes have a marked impact on initiatives to improve progression and continuity. For example, in England specialist schools had to bid for money from government to invest in infrastructure (buildings and equipment) to enhance specific aspects in which they could show curriculum strengths. An important criterion of successful bids was that schools had to show how they would improve KS2/3 transfer in all core subjects, English, Mathematics and Science. More than half of the 60 schools that were trained to use science bridging units at York came because of this. Today the criteria for specialist school bids do not mention transfer or progression-continuity. While annual reports from school inspectors in England (see, for example, Ofsted, 2006; 2007) continue to mention transfer issues, the amount of column inches directed to this has decreased over the past few years as many other priorities have emerged and require comment.

Drawing on the experience, research and reflection on innovation in this book there appear to me to be four basic *conditions* under which better progression and continuity in science might occur:

Condition 1: Learning environment. There is a learning environment in the secondary school that, while not replicating what pupils experienced before, takes on board best practice of primary schools. Actions should include, providing colourful displays relevant to pupils, celebrating work carried out in the first few weeks in the new school, encouraging paired and group discussions and using older pupils to act as working partners or mentors.

Condition 2: Assessment. Assessment at both sides of transfer should be focused on and involve individuals, pairs or groups of pupils drawing on the best practices of formative and diagnostic assessment (for example, as recognized by Black et al.). Pupils should have oral feedback from their teachers about their work as regularly as they did at primary school.

Condition 3: Progression in learning. There has to be recognition that learning science is progressive, building gradually on foundations already laid before. This means recognizing that the journey began some time ago and that it is natural to revisit areas of knowledge to make our thinking better and to have a more complete understanding of the world. The skills and procedures of science are a common tool kit that is expanded as pupils learn and can do more. Teachers must talk to pupils about what they have done before, value their efforts and help them look forward to the next steps in their learning.

Condition 4: Liaison and collaboration. There should be school policies that allow regular high-quality sharing of pedagogy and practice either side of transfers. This means more than just liaison or moderation meetings and induction days. Work either side of transfer can be co-planned using existing bridging units and projects or work of schools' own design. Liaison ought to involve two-way teacher exchanges requiring observation of each other's practices.

Finally, it is worth noting that initiatives, interventions, teaching and training programmes alone, even under the conditions listed above, are not guaranteed success. In the words of Pawson and Tilley (1997: 36):

> it is not programmes which work as such, but people co-operating and choosing to make them work.

Glossary

Admissions Process by which pupils are allocated and admitted to secondary schools. Every secondary school must set a fair and transparent admissions policy which is taken into account in cases of appeals.

Appeals A procedure to resolve problems where the LA has allocated a secondary school place and for some reason parents challenge the decision. The appeal may involve school governors, LA officers, the parents and representatives of the secondary school.

Assessment for Learning (AfL) Assessment for Learning is the process of gathering information about learning, written, oral or visual. This is considered and comments fed back to indicate what the learner should do next in order to make progress. Significantly, this is about formative not summative assessment and is accompanied by a narrative rather than marks or grades.

Attainment targets Programmes of study for the subjects of the National Curriculum are assessed according to criteria set out in attainment targets. In science there are currently four. Attainment Target 1 deals with practical activity and the nature of science and is called *Scientific Enquiry*, Attainment Target 2, *Life Processes and Living Things*, covers biology and environment, Attainment Target 3, *Materials and Their Properties*, covers chemistry and Earth sciences and Attainment Target 4, *Physical Processes*, covers physics and astronomy.

Bridging Programme of planned/shared learning where topics are started in one phase or school and completed in the next one.

Clusters (of schools) Generic term applied to grouping schools on the basis of location or intake arrangements – see also 'family of schools' and 'pyramid (of schools)'.

Comprehensive schools Introduced in the late 1950s and the 1960s as all-ability alternatives to grammar and secondary modern schools (see 'eleven plus'). Most schools in England, Wales and Scotland are of this type. Admissions policies must be equitable and avoid selection of pupils on the basis of their abilities.

Continuity Concerned with the ways in which the educational system facilitates and structures experience to provide sufficient challenge and progress for pupils in a recognizable curricular landscape (such as through key stages, programmes of study and attainment targets).

Core subjects   In England these are currently English, mathematics and science. They must be taught in all key stages.

Eleven plus (11+)   Psychometric tests used to score a population of pupils at age 11 to select those who will go to grammar schools and those who will go to secondary modern schools. Introduced in the 1950s and now only used in a few areas of England and in Northern Ireland (see 'comprehensive schools').

Every Child Matters   Legislation introduced by the UK government to integrate policy and approaches on social, family and health care with educational services.

Family of schools   Usually considered to be one secondary school and its feeder primary schools but could also refer to schools sharing the same religious background; hence families of Roman Catholic or Church of England schools.

Feeder schools   These are the primary schools that send pupils to a particular secondary or middle school at transfer. In England, the number of feeder schools will depend on factors such as the geographic location of the school, its agreed maximum intake (pupil spaces available) and whether it is denominational or religiously endowed.

Form tutor/teacher   There is a tradition in most UK secondary schools that a teacher has overall pastoral responsibility for a form or class. The job is a necessary one as pupils may be taught by a number of different teachers. The form tutor monitors the overall academic progress and behaviour of pupils in their care.

Foundation subjects   National Curriculum subjects which must be taught but are not assessed and reported on nationally, for example, history, geography, art and physical education (PE). Some subjects such as PE must be taught until age 16, others can be optional after age 14.

Induction days   Days held in secondary schools for Y6 pupils who will join secondary schools in the autumn term.

Key stages   The National Curriculum introduced into England and Wales in 1989, and to Northern Ireland in 1991, divided statutory ages of schooling into four 'key stages'. Key Stage 1 (ages 5–7) and Key Stage 2 (ages 7–11) cover the ages in most primary schools. Key Stage 3 (ages 11–14) and Key Stage 4 (ages 14–16) apply in most secondary schools.

Local authorities (LAs)   Regional bodies responsible for local organization of educational services in UK countries.

Learning to Learn   Learning to Learn is about pupils and students understanding the process of learning rather than being recipients of knowledge. It acknowledges that individuals learn in different ways and develops their thinking skills and powers of reflection. Pupils and students develop the skills to apply their knowledge of learning to new situations.

Levels (of attainment)   Criterion-referenced statements describing desirable outcomes in each attainment target at the end of each key stage. The statements are arranged in a hierarchy of levels from 1 to 8 with level 1 representing the simplest and lowest level of attainment. Level 8+ describes exceptional performance above level 8.

Middle schools   Schools that have transfer ages different to the usual one at age 11. The age ranges of these schools are most commonly 8 or 9–13 or 11–14. These schools were common in some areas of the UK in the 1970s and 1980s often as a result of the application of Piaget's stage theory. With the advent of National Curriculum testing at 11 and 14 these schools are being phased out. There will be few left by 2020.

Nvivo   Software used to analyse qualitative data such as responses from interviews with pupils and teachers. Categories of responses are called 'nodes' and are arranged as 'trees' of nodes. In STAY, research teams at York added in SAT performance and other information to work out associations between types of responses and factors such as ability, age, type of school, and so on.

NYASPP   North Yorkshire AstraZeneca Science Pedagogy and Progression project. A flexible approach to progression and continuity where paired tasks are taught either side of transfer. The emphasis is on promoting science as a natural progression rather than pupils thinking that many KS3 topics are repetition of primary work (see SEPTs).

Open evenings   Events held in secondary schools to promote the school at a time when parents are making choices as to which school to send their children.

Processes   These are sets of procedures that deal with the *thinking* and *decision-making* about how to deploy skills. In this way processes link to what are sometimes described as 'thinking skills'. For example measuring temperatures in different places of a classroom requires thinking about what, how and where to measure as well as the skills of reading a thermometer scale. In many places in the book processes are called *process skills*. These include, planning, predicting, measuring, interpreting results and drawing conclusions.

Programme of study Describes the curriculum content and procedural knowledge to be taught at each key stage transfer.

Progression Describes pupils' personal learning journeys through education and the various ways in which they acquire, hone, apply and develop their skills, knowledge and understanding in increasingly challenging situations.

Pupils' passport A device used to encourage transfer of quality information from primary to secondary schools. Typically pupils collect stamps for achievement of various knowledge or skill objectives and continue the process in their secondary schools. Teachers can use pupils' passports to see what has been covered and achieved.

Pyramid (of schools) This usually refers to a structure whereby one large secondary school takes pupils from a number of middle schools who each in turn take pupils from a number of primary schools – hence the shape is like a 'pyramid'. This arrangement is now rare in England.

Roll The number of pupils who are registered as being in a school at any one time – hence 'school roll' or 'number on roll' (NOR) tells you the size of the school.

SAT Standard attainment tests used nationally in England to assess the whole population of pupils in state schools in English, mathematics and science at ages 7, 11 and 14. Science is not tested at age 7. Data are published as numbers of pupils attaining target levels of the National Curriculum (for example, the target for age 11 is level 4). Schools' results are compared with regional (LA) and national averages and used to construct league tables comparing schools (see levels of attainment).

SEPTs Scientific Enquiry Progression Tasks used to promote continuity and progression in science learning for pupils and teachers (see 'NYASPP').

Skills Skills are small-scale or short-term actions, decisions or routines that underpin practical work. For example, reading the scale of a thermometer or the volume of liquid in a measuring cylinder, or setting the right flame on a Bunsen burner to boil a flask of water.

Specialist schools Comprehensive schools that have raised funds matched by government and have been awarded 'specialist school status' in a particular area of expertise such as science, mathematics, the arts, and so on. Specialist schools must offer the full range of National Curriculum teaching and are expected to co-ordinate with other schools in the area, for example, to offer training.

STAY Science Transition AstraZeneca York project which researched, developed and evaluated science bridging work.

Teacher assessments (TAs) Assessment of pupils' attainments in National Curriculum subjects by teachers against criterion referenced 'levels of attainment'. Reported to parents at the and of each key stage but not used in league tables of schools' performance (see also 'attainment targets', 'levels (of attainment)', 'SATs').

Transfer Transitions in education where there is a major change of location or school, for example, from infant to junior school, primary to secondary school, secondary school to college, secondary school/college to university, or home-based education into the school system.

Transition Key positions in educational life when learning may be subject to change or even disruption. They can be major transitions from one key stage to another or more minor such as from one topic to another.

References

Adams, T. (2007) 'The new age of ignorance', *Observer* Review, page 6, 1 July.

Adey, P. and Shayer, M. (1994) *Really Raising Standards. Cognitive Intervention and Academic Achievement.* London: Routledge.

Adey, P.S., Shayer, M. and Yates, C. (1989) *Thinking Science: Student and Teachers' Materials for the CASE Intervention.* London: Nelson.

Alexander, R.J., Rose, A.J. and Woodhead, C. (1992) *Curriculum organisation and Classroom Practice in Primary Schools, a Discussion Paper.* London: Department of Education and Science.

Anderson, L.W., Jacobs, J., Schramm, S. and Splittberger, F. (2000) 'School transitions: beginning of the end or a new beginning?', *International Journal of Educational Research*, 33: 325–39.

Archenhold, F. (ed.) (1988) *Science at Age 15: A Review of APU Survey Findings 1980–1984.* London: Her Majesty's Stationery Office.

Asoko, H. and Squires, A. (1998) 'Progression and continuity', in M. Ratcliffe (ed.), *ASE Guide to Secondary Science.* Hatfield: Association for Science Education. pp. 175–82.

Association for Science Education (ASE) (1999) *Science and the Literacy Hour: Executive Summary.* Hatfield: Association for Science Education.

Association for Science Education (ASE) (2002) *Science Year CD-ROMs – Who Am I?* Hatfield: Association for Science Education. www.sycd.co.uk/ (accessed 5 June 2007).

Barber, M. and Mourshed, M. (2007) *How the World's Best-Performing School Systems Come Out on Top.* Dubai: McKinsey and Company.

Barnes, D. and Todd, F. (1995) *Communication and Learning Revisited.* London: Heinemann.

Bennett, J. (2003) *Teaching and Learning Science: A Guide to Recent Research and its Applications.* London: Continuum.

Bennett, J., Burden, J., Campbell, P., Millar, R., Osborne, J. and Swinbank, E. (2006) *Looking Forward: Making Key Stage 3 Science Work.* York: Centre for Innovation and Research in Science Education, University of York.

Bennett, J., Hogarth S. and Lubben, F. (2003) 'A systematic review of the effects of context-based and Science-Technology-Society (STS) approaches in the teaching of secondary science', in *Research Evidence in Education Library.* London: EPPI-Centre, Social Science Research Unit, Institute of Education.

Bishop, K. and Denley, P. (2003) 'Primary-secondary transfer: innovative projects to ease transition', *Education in Science*, 202: 8–10.

Black, P. and Wiliam, D. (1998) *Inside the Black Box.* London: King's College, Department of Educational Studies.

Black, P. and Wiliam, D. (2005) 'Lessons from around the world: how policies, politics and cultures constrain and afford assessment practices', *The Curriculum Journal*, 16(2): 249–61.

Black, P., Harrison, C., Lee, C., Marshall, B. and Wiliam, D. (2002) *Working Inside the Black Box: Assessment for Learning in the Classroom.* London: King's College, Department of Education and Professional Studies.

Braund, M. (1996) 'Moratorium on change; an opportunity to reflect on practical work in primary science', in V. Quinn (ed.), *Occasional Papers in The Arts and Education.* Vol. 7. Wakefield/Bretton Hall: The National Arts and Education Archive. pp. 51–70.

Braund, M. (2002) 'STAYing the course: smoothing the transfer from Key Stage 2 to Key Stage 3', *Education in Science*, 197, 28–9.

Braund, M. (2006) 'Research focus: Key Stage 2/3 transfer in science: what research has to say', *Education in Science*, 218: 26–7.

Braund, M. (2007) '"Bridging work" and its role in improving progression and continuity: an example from science education', *British Educational Research Journal*, 33(6): 905–26.

Braund, M. (forthcoming) 'Curriculum development in the United Kingdom: themes, trends and tensions', in J. Kirlo and A. Naumann (eds), *Curriculum Development: Perspectives from Around the World*. Louisiana: Association of Childhood Education (ACEI).

Braund, M. and Driver, M. (2005a) 'Pupils' perceptions of practical science in primary and secondary school: implications for improving progression and continuity of learning', *Educational Research*, 47(1): 77–91.

Braund, M. and Driver, M. (2005b) *STAYing the Course. Improving KS2/3 Transfer in Science*. 2nd edn. York: University of York Science Education Group.

Braund, M. and Hames, V. (2005) 'Improving progression and continuity from primary to secondary science: pupils' reactions to bridging work', *International Journal of Science Education*, 27(7): 781–801.

Braund, M. and Reiss, M. (2006) 'Validity and worth in the science curriculum: learning school science outside the laboratory', *The Curriculum Journal*, 17(3): 313–28.

Braund, M., Crompton, Z., Driver, M. and Parvin, J. (2003) 'Bridging the key stage gap in science', *School Science Review*, 85(310): 117–23.

Braund, M., Greenway, T. and Crompton, Z. (eds) (2004) *Moving On. Scientific Enquiry Progression Tasks for KS2 and KS3*. Northallerton: The North Yorkshire AstraZeneca Science Pedagogy and Progression (NYASPP) Project, North Yorkshire County Council Education Service.

Braund, M., Parvin, J., Hall, A. and Early, R. (2007) 'Talking science in the primary school: researching classroom environments and pupils' attitudes and learning efficacies', paper presented at the conference of the Australasian Science Education Research Association, Fremantle, Western Australia, 11–14 July.

Brighouse, T. and Woods, D. (2006) *Inspirations: A Collection of Commentaries to Promote School Improvement*. London: Network Continuum.

Bruner, J. (1960) *The Process of Education*. Cambridge, MA: Harvard University Press.

Bruner, J. (1966) *Toward a Theory of Instruction*. Cambridge, MA: Belkapp Press.

Bunyan, P. (1998) 'Comparing pupil performance in Key Stages 2 and 3 science SATs', *School Science Review*, 79(289): 85–7.

Campbell, B., Lazonby, J., Millar, R. and Smith, S. (1990) *Science, the Salters' Approach: Books 1–4*. Oxford: Heinemann.

Campbell, R., Bennett, J., Braund, M. and McGuinn, N. (2005) *Trainee Teachers' Responses to Systematic Review Reports of Educational Research in the Areas of English and Science. Departmental Research Papers No 10*. York: Department of Educational Studies, University of York.

Central Advisory Council for Education (CACE) (1967) *Children and their Primary Schools*. (Plowden report.) London: HMSO.

Cheshire County Council (n.d.) *Bridging the Gap. KS2/3 Liaison – Bubbles*. Cheshire: Zeneca Pharmaceuticals in partnership with Cheshire Inspection and Advisory Service, Cheshire County Council.

Coe, R. (2002) 'It's the effect size, stupid: what effect size is and why it is important', paper presented at the British Educational Research Association annual conference, Exeter, 12–14 September. www.leeds.ac.uk/educol/documents/00002182.htm (accessed 4 February 2005).

Cohen, J. (1969) *Statistical Power Analysis for the Behavioural Sciences*. New York: Academic Press.

Consortium of Local Education Authorities for the Provision of Science Services (CLEAPSS) (2001) *CLEAPSS Laboratory Handbook, Guidance on Microbiology Section 15.2*. Uxbridge: CLEAPSS.

Cordingley, P., Bell, M., Rundell, B. and Evans, D. (2003) 'The impact of collaborative CPD on classroom teaching and learning', in *Research Evidence in Education Library*. London: EPPI-Centre, Social Science Research Unit, Institute of Education.

Corrie, C. (2003) *Becoming Emotionally Intelligent*. Stafford: Network Continuum Education.

Cosh, J. (1999) 'Peer observation: a reflective model', *ELT journal*, 53(1): 22–7.

Cowie, H. and Wallace, P. (2000) *Peer Support in Action: From Bystanding to Standing By*. London: Sage Publications.

Cox, C.B. and Dyson, A.E. (eds) (1969a) *Fight for Education: A Black Paper*. Manchester: Critical Quarterly Society.

Cox, C.B. and Dyson, A.E. (eds) (1969b) *Black Paper 2: The Crisis in Education*. Manchester: Critical Quarterly Society.

Craig, J. and Ayers, D. (1988) 'Does primary science affect girls' and boys' interest in secondary science', *School Science Review*, 69(3): 417–26.

Crebbin, C. (2001) 'Partnership teaching in primary science', *Primary Science Review*, 70: 22–5.

Curran, A. (2006) 'How the "brian" works', in I. Gilbert (ed.), *The Big Book of Independent Thinking*. Carmarthen: Crown House. pp. 113–36.

Davies, D., and McMahon, K. (2004) 'A smooth trajectory: developing continuity and progression between primary and secondary science education through a jointly-planned projectiles project', *International Journal of Science Education*, 26(8): 1009–21.

Department for Education and Employment and the Qualifications and Curriculum Authority (DfEE/QCA) (1999) *Science: The National Curriculum for England*. London: QCA.

Department for Education and Employment and the Qualifications and Curriculum Authority (DfEE/QCA) (2000a) *A Scheme of Work for Key Stages 1 and 2: Science*. London: QCA.

Department for Education and Employment and the Qualifications and Curriculum Authority (DfEE/QCA) (2000b) *Science. A scheme of work for Key Stage 3*. London: QCA.

Department for Education and Employment (DfEE) and the Teacher Training Agency (TTA) (1998a) *Initial Teacher Training National Curriculum for Primary Science (Annexe E of DfEE Circular 4/98)*. London: DfEE/TTA.

Department for Education and Employment (DfEE) and the Teacher Training Agency (TTA) (1998b) *Initial Teacher Training National Curriculum for Secondary Science (Annexe E of DfEE Circular 4/98)*. London: DfEE/TTA.

Department for Education and Skills (DfES) (2002a) *English Transition Units*. London: Department for Education and Skills. Crown Copyright.

Department for Education and Skills (DfES) (2002b) *Supporting Transition From Year 6 to Year 7 Science. Course Pack for Tutors. Key Stage 3 National Strategy Training Materials*. London: Department for Education and Skills.

Department for Education and Skills (DfES) (2003) *Mathematics Transition Units – 2003 Edition*. London: Department for Education and Skills. Crown Copyright.

Department for Education and Skills (DfES) (2005) *Excellence and Enjoyment: Social and Emotional Aspects of Learning. New Beginnings Theme Overview Booklet*. London: DfES. www.standards.dfes.gov.uk/primary/publications/banda/seal/ (accessed 9 September 2007).

Department of Education and Science/Welsh Office (DES/WO) (1985) *Science 5–16: A Statement of Policy*. London: Department of Education and Science and the Welsh Office.

Department of Education and Science/Welsh Office (DES/WO) (1988a) *National Curriculum: Task Group on Assessment and Testing: A Report*. London: Department of Education and Science and the Welsh Office.

Department of Education and Science and the Welsh Office (DES/WO) (1988b) *Science for Ages 5 to 16 (Final Report of the Science Working Group)*. London: Her Majesty's Stationery Office.

Department of Education and Science and the Welsh Office (DES/WO) (1989) *Science in the National Curriculum*. London: Her Majesty's Stationery Office.

Derricott, R. (ed.) (1985) *Curriculum Continuity: Primary to Secondary*. Windsor: National Foundation for Educational Research (NFER)-Nelson.

Dobson, K. (1987) *Coordinated Science, the Suffolk Development, Teachers' Handbook*. London: Collins.

Donnelly, J. (2000) 'Secondary science teaching under the National Curriculum', *School Science Review*, 81(296): 27–37.

Doyle, L. and Hetherington, N. (1998). 'Learning progression across the primary/secondary divide', *All-in Success (Journal of the Centre for The Study of Comprehensive Schools [CSCS])*, 9(2): 9–12.

Driver, R., Guesne, E. and Tiberghien, A. (eds) (1985) *Children's Ideas in Science*. Milton Keynes: Open University Press.

Dutch, R. and McCall, J. (1974) 'Transition to secondary – an experiment in a Scottish comprehensive school'. *British Journal of Educational Psychology*, 44(3): 282–89.

Eccles, J.S. and Midgley, C. (1989). 'Stage-Environment Fit: Developmentally Appropriate Classrooms for Young Adolescents', in C. Ames and R. Ames (eds), *Research on Motivation in Education. Volume 3: Goals and Cognitions*. London: Academic Press. pp. 139–86.

Every Child Matters. www.everychildmatters.gov.uk (accessed, 3 December 2007).

Galton, M. (2002) 'Continuity and progression in science teaching at Key Stages 2 and 3', *Cambridge Journal of Education*, 32(2): 250–65.

Galton, M. and MacBeath, J. (2002) *A Life in Teaching? The Impact of Change on Primary Teachers' Working Lives*. Cambridge: Faculty of Education, University of Cambridge.

Galton, M., Edwards, J., Hargreaves, L. and Pell, T. (2003a) 'Continuities and discontinuities at transfer', in M. Galton, G. Gray, and J. Rudduck (eds), *Transfer and Transitions in the Middle Years of Schooling (7–14): Continuities and Discontinuities in Learning*. Nottingham: Department for Education and Skills.

Galton, M., Gray, J. and Rudduck, J. (1999) *The Impact of School Transitions and Transfers on Pupil Progress and Attainment. Research Report RR 131*. London: Department for Education and Employment.

Galton, M., Gray, G. and Rudduck, J. (2003b) *Transfer and Transitions in the Middle Years of Schooling, 7–14: Continuities and Discontinuities in Learning*. Nottingham: Department for Education and Skills.

Galton, M., Hargreaves, L. and Pell, T. (2003c) 'Progress in the middle years of schooling: continuities and discontinuities at transfer', *Education 3–13*, June: 9–18.

Galton, M., Simon, B. and Croll, P. (1980) *Inside the Primary Classroom*. London: Routledge.

Gardner, H. (2001) 'Jerome S. Bruner', in J.A. Palmer (ed.), *Fifty Modern Thinkers on Education. From Piaget to the Present*. London: Routledge.

Gilbert, I. (2005) *Essential Motivation in the Classroom*. Oxford: RoutledgeFalmer.

Glass, G.V., McGaw, B. and Smith, M.L. (1981) *Meta-analysis in Social Research*. London: Sage Publications.

Goldsworthy, A., Watson, R. and Wood-Robinson, V. (2000) *AKSIS, Developing Understanding in Scientific Enquiry*. Hatfield: ASE.

Goleman, D. (1996) *Emotional Intelligence: Why It Can Matter More than IQ*. London: Bloomsbury.

Goodrum, D., Hackling, M. and Rennie, L. (2001) *The Status and Quality of Teaching and Learning of Science in Australian Schools*. Canberra: Commonwealth Department of Education, Training and Youth Affairs.

Gorwood, B. (1994) 'Primary–secondary transfer after the National Curriculum', in R. Moon and A.S. Mayes (eds), *Teaching and Learning in the Secondary School*. London: Routledge.

Gott, R. and Duggan, S. (1995) *Investigative Work in the Science Curriculum*. Buckingham: Open University Press.

Graham, D. (1993) *A lesson for as all: The making of the National Curriculum*. London: Routledge.

Hall, I., Lin, M., Smith, P. and Todd, L. (2001) *Beacon Council Research – Round 3 Theme Report. Transition in Education: Transition Between Key Stages in Schools*. Newcastle: Department of Education, University of Newcastle-upon-Tyne.

Hargreaves, D. (1996) *Teaching as a Research-Based Profession: Possibilities and Prospects*. Teacher Training Agency Annual Lecture. London: Teacher Training Agency.

Hargreaves, L. and Galton, M. (2002) *Transfer From the Primary Classroom: 20 Years On*. London: Routledge and Falmer.

Harlen, W. (1996) *The Teaching of Science in the Primary School*. 2nd Edn. London: Fulton.

Harlen, W. and Jelly, S. (1997) *Developing Science in the Primary Classroom*. Harlow: Longman.

Hodson, D. (1988) 'Towards a philosophically more valid science curriculum', *Science Education*, 14: 31–62.

House of Commons Education Committee (1995) *Fourth Report: Science and Technology in Schools*. London: HMSO.

House of Lords (2006) *Science Teaching in Schools: 10th Report of the Science and Technology Committee*. London: The Stationery Office.

Inner London Education Authority (ILEA) (1987) *Science in Process*. London: Heinemann.

Jarman, R. (1990) 'Primary science-secondary science continuity: a new ERA?', *School Science Review*, 71(257): 19–29.

Jarman, R. (1993) 'Real experiments with Bunsen burners: pupils' perceptions of the similarities and differences between primary science and secondary science', *School Science Review*, 74 (268): 19–29.

Jarman, R. (1997) 'Fine in theory: a study of primary–secondary continuity in science, prior and subsequent to the introduction of the Northern Ireland Curriculum', *Educational Research*, 39(3): 291–310.

Jenkins, E.W. (2000) 'The impact of the national curriculum on secondary school science teaching in England and Wales', *International Journal of Science Education*, 22(3): 325–36.

Jensen, E. (1995) *The Learning Brain*. San Diego, CA: The Brain Store.

Keogh, B. and Naylor, S. (1999) 'Concept cartoons, teaching and learning in science: an evaluation', *International Journal of Science Education*, 21(4): 431–46.

Kerry, T. and Eggleston, J. (1994) 'The evolution of the topic', in A.D. and J. Bourne (eds) *Teaching and Learning in the Primary School*. London: Routledge. pp.188–93.

Keys, W., Harris, S. and Fernandes, C. (1995) *Attitudes to School of Top Primary and First-Year Secondary Pupils*. Slough: National Foundation for Educational Research.

Lee, B., Harris, S. and Dickson, P. (1995) *Continuity and Progression 5–16: Developments in Schools*. Slough: National Foundation for Educational Research/Nelson.

Lipsey, M.W. and Wilson, D.B. (1993) 'The efficacy of psychological, educational and behavioural treatment: confirmation from meta-analysis', *American Psychologist*, 48(12): 1181–209.

Marland, M. and Rogers, R. (1997) *The Art of the Tutor: Developing Your Role in the Secondary School*. London: David Fulton.

Martin, M., Mullis, I., Gonzalez, E., Gregory, K., Smith, T., Chrostowski, S., Garden, R. and O'Connor, K. (2000) *TIMSS 1999 International Science Report Findings from IEA's Report of the Third International Mathematics and Science Study at Eighth Grade.* Boston, MA: International Study Center, Lynch School of Education, International Association for the Evaluation of Educational Achievement.

Maslow, A.H. (1987) *Motivation and Personality.* 3rd edition. New York: Harper and Row.

Millar, R. (2006) 'Twenty first century science: insights from the design and implementation of a scientific literacy approach in school science', *International Journal of Science Education*, 28(13): 1499–521.

Millar, R. and Driver, R. (1987) 'Beyond processes', *Studies in Science Education*, 72: 19–40.

Millar, R. and Osborne, J. (eds) (1998) *Beyond 2000: Science Education for the Future* London: King's College, School of Education.

Millar, R., Holman, J., Hunt, A., Lazonby, J., Milner, B., and Reiss, M. (2001) *QCA Key Stage 4 Curriculum Models Project. Final Report.* York: University of York Science Education Group.

Morrison, I. (2000) 'School's great – apart from the lessons: sustaining the excitement of learning post transfer', *Improving Schools*, 3(1): 46–9.

National Curriculum Council (NCC) (1991) *NCC Inset Resources: Science Explorations.* York: National Curriculum Council.

Newton, L. and Newton, D. (1998) 'Primary children's conceptions of science and the scientist: is the impact of a National Curriculum breaking down the stereotype?', *International Journal of Science Education*, 20(9): 1137–49.

Nicholls, G. and Gardner, J. (1999) *Pupils in Transition Moving between Key Stages.* London: Routledge.

Nott, M. and Wellington, J. (1999) 'The state we're in: issues in Key Stage 3 and 4 science', *School Science Review*, 81(294): 13–18.

Office for Standards in Education (Ofsted) (2002a) *Good Teaching, Effective Departments: Findings from an HMI Survey of Subject Teaching in Secondary Schools, 2000/01.* London: Office for Standards in Education. www.ofsted.gov.uk (accessed 4 August, 2006).

Office for Standards in Education (Ofsted) (2002b) *Changing Schools: An Evaluation of Effectiveness of Transfer Arrangements at Age 11.* www.ofsted.gov.uk/public/docs02/changingschoolsreport.pdf. 3rd July 2002 (accessed 4 August, 2006).

Office for Standards in Education (Ofsted) (2004a) *A New Relationship with Schools: Improving Performance through School Self-Evaluation.* London: Department for Education and Skills.

Office for Standards in Education (Ofsted) (2004b) *The Key Stage 3 Strategy: Evaluation of the Third Year.* London: Office for Standards in Education.

Office for Standards in Education (Ofsted) (2005) *Every Child Matters: Framework for the Inspection of Schools from 2005.* London: The Stationery Office.

Office for Standards in Education (Ofsted) (2006) *The Annual Report of Her Majesty's Chief Inspector of Schools 2005/6.* London: The Stationery Office.

Office for Standards in Education (Ofsted) (2007) *The annual report of Her Majesty's Chief Inspector for Education, Children's Services and Schools, 2006–7.* London: Office for Standards in Education: The Stationery Office.

Osborne, J. and Collins, S. (2001) 'Pupils' views of the role and value of the science curriculum: a focus-group study', *International Journal of Science Education*, 23(5): 441–67.

Osborne, R. and Freyburg, P. (1985) *Learning in Science: The Implications of Children's Science*, Auckland: Heinemann.

Pawson, R. and Tilley, N. (1997) *Realistic Evaluation.* London: Sage Publications.

Peacock, G. (1999) 'Continuity and progression between key stages in science', paper presented to the conference of the British Educational Research Association, University of Sussex, 2–5 September.

Pell, T. and Jarvis, T. (2001) 'Developing attitude to science scales for use with children of ages from five to eleven years', *International Journal of Science Education*, 33(8): 847–62.

Pietarinen, J. (2000) 'Transfer to and study at secondary school in Finnish school culture: developing schools on the basis of pupils' experiences', *International Journal of Educational Research*, 33: 383–400.

Pointon, P. (2000) 'Students' views of environments for learning from primary to secondary school', *International Journal of Educational Research*, 33: 375–82.

Primary Science Review (2007) 'All change or small change?', *Primary Science Review*, 100: 9–13.

Primary Review (2007a) *The Primary Interim Reports: Community Soundings, Regional Witness Sessions*. Cambridge: University of Cambridge (accessed 4 November 2007).

Primary Review (2007b) *The Primary Review Briefings: Community Soundings, Regional Witness Sessions*. Cambridge: University of Cambridge. www.primaryreview.org. uk/Downloads/Int_Reps/1.Com_Sdg/Primary_Review_Community_Soundings_ briefing_final.pdf (accessed 22 November 2007).

Qualifications and Curriculum Authority (QCA) (2000) *Bridging Units in Mathematics: Algebra Introducing Symbols*. Sudbury: Qualifications and Curriculum Authority (QCA) Publications.

Qualifications and Curriculum Authority (QCA) (2007a) 'The aims of the curriculum (as part of national curriculum 2008)'. London: QCA. http://curriculum.qca.org. uk/(accessed 23 November 2007).

Qualifications and Curriculum Authority (QCA) (2007b) 'Science programmes of study and attainment targets (as part of national curriculum 2008)'. London: QCA. http:// curriculum. qca.org.uk/subjects/science/keystage3 (accessed 23 November 2007).

Qualter, A., Strang, J., Swatton, P., and Taylor, R. (1990) *Exploration: A Way of Learning Science*. Oxford: Blackwell.

Reiss, M. (2000) *Understanding Science Lessons. Five Years of Science Teaching*. Buckingham: Open University Press.

Roderick, M. and Camburn, E. (1999) 'Risk and recovery from course failure in the early years of high school', *American Educational Research Journal*, 36(2): 303–43.

Roker, D. and Shepard, J. (2003) *Supporting Children and Parents during the Transition to Secondary School: A UK-wide Review*. Brighton: Trust for the Study of Adolescence. www.studyofadolescence.org.uk/research/projects (accessed 16 September 2007).

Roth, W.-M. (1997) 'From everyday science to science education: how science and technology inspired curriculum design and classroom research', *Science and Education*, 6: 373–96.

Royal Society (2006a) *Taking a Leading Role – Scientists Survey*. London: The Royal Society. www.royalsoc.ac.uk/page.asp?id=2903 (accessed 21 November 2006).

Royal Society (2006b) *Increasing the Uptake of Science post-16*. London: The Royal Society.

Rudduck, J., Chaplain, R. and Wallace, G. (1996) 'Pupil voices and school improvement', in J. Rudduck, R. Chaplain and G. Wallace (eds), *School Improvement: What Can Pupils Tell Us?* London: David Fulton.

Russell, T. (ed.) (1988) *Science at Age 11: A Review of APU Survey Findings 1980–1984*. London: Her Majesty's Stationery Office.

Schagen, S. and Kerr, D. (1999) *Bridging The Gap? The National Curriculum and Progression from Primary to Secondary School*. Slough: Nuffield Foundation for Educational Research.

Scharf, P.F. and Schibeci, R.A. (1990) 'The influence of a "transition science" unit on student attitudes', *Research in Science and Technological Education*, 8: 79–88.

Schofield, B. (ed.) (1989) *Science at Age 13: A Review of APU Survey Findings 1980–1984*. London: Her Majesty's Stationery Office.

Schön, D. (1983) *The Reflective Practitioner: How Professionals Think in Action.* London: Basic Books.

Schön, D. (1987) *Educating the Reflective Practitioner: toward a New Design for Teaching and Learning in the Professions.* San Francisco, CA: Jossey-Bass.

Screen, P. (1986) *Warwick Process Science.* Southampton: Ashford Press.

Secondary Science Curriculum Review (SSCR) (1987) *Better Science: Building Primary–Secondary Links,* London: Heinemann.

Sjøberg, S. (1997) 'Scientific literacy and school science', in S. Sjøberg and E. Kallerud (eds), *Science Technology and Citizenship: The Public Understanding of Science and Technology in Science Education and Research Policy.* Oslo: Norwegian Institute for Studies in Research and Higher Education.

Snow, C.P. (1993) *The Two Cultures.* Cambridge: Cambridge University Press.

Speering, W. and Rennie, L. (1996) 'Students' perceptions about science: the impact of transition from primary to secondary school', *Research in Science Education,* 26(3): 283–98.

Stenhouse, L. (1971) 'The humanities curriculum project: the rationale', *Theory into Practice,* 10(3): 154–62.

Stillman, A. and Maychell, K. (1984) School to School: LEA and Teacher Involvement in Educational Continuity. Windsor: NFER-Nelson.

Stoll, L., Stobart, G., Martin, S., Freeman, S., Freedman, S., Sammons, P. and Smees, R. (2003) *Preparing for Change: Evaluation of the Implementation of the Key Stage 3 Strategy Pilot.* Bath: Nottingham: Department for Education and Skills, University of Bath.

Stringer, J. (2003) 'We've all done this before', *Primary Science Review,* 80: 4–6.

Suffolk Education Department (1996) *A Report of an Investigation into What Happens When Pupils Transfer into their Next Schools at the Ages of 9, 11 and 13.* Ipswich: Inspection and Advice Division, Suffolk Education Department.

Suffolk County Council Education Department (2002a) *Transfer Review 2001 – Summary.* Ipswich: Suffolk County Council.

Suffolk County Council Education Department (2002b) *Transfer Review 2001 Annex C – Summary of the Findings for Science.* Ipswich: Suffolk County Council.

Teacher Training Agency (TTA) (2000a) *Initial Teacher Training National Curriculum for Secondary Science, Annex H of DfEE circular 4/98.* London: Teacher Training Agency.

Teacher Training Agency (TTA) (2000b) *Initial Teacher Training National Curriculum for Primary Science, Annex E of DfEE circular 4/98.* London: Teacher Training Agency.

Teach First (2007) *Lessons from the Front.* London: Teach First.

The Children Act 2004. www.opsi.gov.uk/acts2004 (accessed 3 December 2007).

Watson, R. and Wood-Robinson, V. (1998) 'Learning to investigate', in M. Ratcliffe (ed.), *ASE Guide to Secondary Science.* Hatfield: ASE. pp. 92–9.

Woods, P. (1986) *Inside Schools. Ethnography in Educational Research.* London: Routledge.

Useful Websites

The AstraZeneca Science Teaching Trust   www.azteachscience.co.uk/

The Professional Development Unit on the AZSTT website with details of lesson plans, how to use planning posters and much more from the STAY project can be viewed online or downloaded from   www.azteachscience.co.uk/code/development/stay.asp

This website holds information on over 80 transition and transfer projects in the UK and is connected to Maurice Galton's research   http://creict.homerton.cam.ac.uk/transfer/

Index

Entries in **bold** type refer to the key points for the subject in the book.

Research Methods Books
from SAGE

Action Research
in the Classroom

Vivienne Baumfield, Elaine Hall & Kate Wall

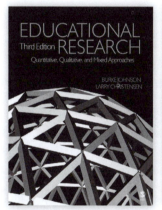

EDUCATIONAL
Third Edition RESEARCH
Quantitative, Qualitative, and Mixed Approaches

BURKE JOHNSON
LARRY CHRISTENSEN

Doing Your
EDUCATION
RESEARCH
PROJECT

Neil Burton
Mark Brundrett
Marion Jones

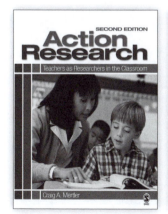

SECOND EDITION
Action
Research
Teachers as Researchers in the Classroom

Craig A. Mertler

Researching
with Children & Research,
Design Methods
Young People and Analysis

Kay Tisdell, John Davis
& Michael Gallagher

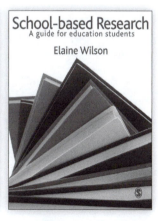

School-based Research
A guide for education students

Elaine Wilson

www.sagepub.co.uk/education

Research Methods Books from SAGE

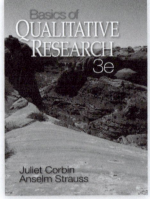

Basics of QUALITATIVE RESEARCH 3e

Juliet Corbin
Anselm Strauss

The Mixed Methods Reader

Vicki L. Plano Clark ■ John W. Creswell

DOING QUALITATIVE RESEARCH USING YOUR COMPUTER

A PRACTICAL GUIDE

CHRIS HAHN

SECOND EDITION
INTERVIEWS
Learning the Craft of Qualitative Research Interviewing

Steinar Kvale
Svend Brinkmann

DISCOVERING STATISTICS USING SPSS THIRD EDITION

ANDY FIELD

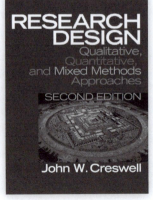

RESEARCH DESIGN
Qualitative, Quantitative, and Mixed Methods Approaches
SECOND EDITION

John W. Creswell